Practical Web Design

Learn the fundamentals of web design with HTML5, CSS3, Bootstrap, jQuery, and Vue.js

Philippe Hong

BIRMINGHAM - MUMBAI

Practical Web Design

Commissioning Editor: Kunal Chaudhari
Acquisition Editor: Nigel Fernandes
Content Development Editor: Arun Nadar
Technical Editor: Surabhi Kulkarni
Copy Editor: Safis Editing
Project Coordinator: Sheejal Shah
Proofreader: Safis Editing
Indexer: Mariammal Chettiyar
Graphics: Jason Monteiro
Production Coordinator: Shantanu Zagade

First published: April 2018

Production reference: 1240418

Published by Packt Publishing Ltd.
Livery Place
35 Livery Street
Birmingham
B3 2PB, UK.

ISBN 978-1-78839-503-8

www.packtpub.com

`mapt.io`

Mapt is an online digital library that gives you full access to over 5,000 books and videos, as well as industry leading tools to help you plan your personal development and advance your career. For more information, please visit our website.

Why subscribe?

- Spend less time learning and more time coding with practical eBooks and Videos from over 4,000 industry professionals

- Improve your learning with Skill Plans built especially for you

- Get a free eBook or video every month

- Mapt is fully searchable

- Copy and paste, print, and bookmark content

PacktPub.com

Did you know that Packt offers eBook versions of every book published, with PDF and ePub files available? You can upgrade to the eBook version at `www.PacktPub.com` and as a print book customer, you are entitled to a discount on the eBook copy. Get in touch with us at `service@packtpub.com` for more details.

At `www.PacktPub.com`, you can also read a collection of free technical articles, sign up for a range of free newsletters, and receive exclusive discounts and offers on Packt books and eBooks.

Contributers

About the author

Philippe Hong is a French award-winning designer, UI/UX, and front-end developer. He's a creative person who's passionate about making the best possible experience for people. The judge at CSSDA, he won several awards, such as *two Website of the day* awards, *Bemyapp Games WorldCup*, *Dailymotion Best Mobile application,* and many others. He has had the privilege to work with well-known brands and is an actively engaged designer who takes pleasure in writing and talking about design on different occasions.

> *I want to particularly thank my partner Vivienne. Without her, I wouldn't have been able to do this—thanks for all the encouragement and for reviewing my texts. Thanks also to my family and friends, who supported and encouraged me in this endeavor.*

About the reviewers

Marija Zaric is a freelance web designer living in Belgrade, Serbia, with a focus on individual and commercial clients who demand websites that are modern, creative, simple, and responsive. She works with clients from the USA and all over the world, helping them present their services in a unique and professional way. Marija was a technical reviewer for the books *Responsive Media in HTML5*, *Mastering Responsive Web Design*, *Responsive Web Design Patterns*, and *Mastering Bootstrap 4* for Packt Publishing.

Kang Hong Chen is an artist and developer currently based in London, UK. He has previously worked on the core development team of Airtasker, ustwo, and now is working at Net a Porter. He has collaborated with Philippe on design system software such as Sketch Export Generator. Ed blogs at edsnider [dot] net and can be found on Twitter at twitter [dot] com/edsnider.

Packt is searching for authors like you

If you're interested in becoming an author for Packt, please visit `authors.packtpub.com` and apply today. We have worked with thousands of developers and tech professionals, just like you, to help them share their insight with the global tech community. You can make a general application, apply for a specific hot topic that we are recruiting an author for, or submit your own idea.

Table of Contents

Preface   1

Chapter 1: Evolution of Web Design   7
The first ever website   8
Table-based layouts   10
Introduction of Flash   12
CSS – the savior   14
Web 2.0   16
The rise of the mobile   17
Responsive web design   18
Flat design   19
What's next?   22
Summary   22

Chapter 2: Web Design and its Components   23
Grids   24
  The cons   25
Call to Action   27
  Making it obvious   27
  Using contrasting color   29
  Compelling copy   30
  Placement   31
Breadcrumb   32
The search bar   34
  The submit button   34
  Making it noticeable   35
  Placing the search bar correctly   37
Icons   37
  Describing in a nutshell   38
  Drawing attention of the users   38
  Directional   40
Modal   40
Typography   43
  Choosing a font that connects your brand   44
    Serif fonts   44
    Sans-serif   45
    Casual scripts   46
  Don't use too much typeface   46
Colors   50

What colors mean	50
Usability	52
Simplicity	53
Navigability	53
Accessibility	54
Consistency	55
So, how can we be consistent?	55
Design	56
Content	57
Interactions	57
Summary	57
Chapter 3: Website-Designing Workflow	59
Our situation	59
Goal identification	59
What is the purpose of the website?	60
Who is the website for?	60
Is this useful for our audience?	60
What do they expect to find or do there?	60
Does the website need to follow a brand or have its own brand identity?	61
Are there any competitors? If there are, how is the website different than others?	61
Defining the scope	62
Creating wireframes	62
Designing	66
Get inspiration	66
Improve	66
Invent	66
Implementing, testing, and launching	68
Summary	68
Chapter 4: Responsive Versus Adaptive Design	69
Responsive design	70
Adaptive design	73
So which one is the best?	76
The takeaway	78
Summary	78
Chapter 5: Learning HTML5	79
Our main tool	79
What is HTML?	81
HTML tags	81
HTML attributes	82
HTML structure	82
Creating our first page	82

HTML elements 83
   Titles and paragraphs 83
   Links and images 86
Summary 89
Chapter 6: Learning CSS3 91
  The different ways to use CSS 91
  CSS formatting 92
  Parent and child elements 93
  Classes and IDs 94
  CSS box model 97
    The boxes 97
    Block and inline 99
  CSS layout and dividers 101
    The basic layout 101
    Formatting and indenting your HTML 102
    Styling our class 102
  Summary 110
Chapter 7: Building Your Own Website 111
  Our design 111
  Installing HTML Boilerplate 113
    Editing index.html 115
  Creating our web page 117
    Images folder 118
    Installing our font 118
    Importing Google Font 120
    Adding normalize.css 121
  The header 121
    Creating a menu 121
    Inserting links 122
    Adding a logo 123
    Right-hand side menu 124
    Adding a Facebook like button 124
    Styling our header 126
  Adding the hero section 135
    CSS flexbox 141
    Positioning in CSS 143
      Position static 144
      Position relative 144
      Position absolute 144
      Position fixed 145
      Position sticky 146
  Blog section 147
  Creating the ABOUT US section 156

Adding the Partner section   163
Adding the footer section   168
Summary   172
Chapter 8: Making Our Website Responsive   173
    What are media queries?   174
       Opening the inspector   175
       Desktop first   178
    Designing the menu   179
    What is jQuery?   188
       jQuery syntax   189
    Making the hero section responsive   194
    Making the Blog section responsive   195
    Making the ABOUT US section responsive   198
    Making the footer section responsive   200
    Summary   202
Chapter 9: Adding Interaction and Dynamic Content   203
    CSS pseudo-classes   203
    Sticky navigation   206
       JS Plugin: Waypoints   209
       CSS animation   211
    Adding a dynamic Instagram feed   213
       Installing Instafeed.js   215
       Getting images from your user account   216
       Finding our userID and TokenAccess   217
       Getting our access token   219
       Displaying the feed   223
    Summary   232
Chapter 10: Optimizing and Launching Our Website   233
    Creating a favicon   233
    Site performance optimization   236
       Optimizing images   237
       Optimizing our code   238
    Basic SEO improvement   239
       What is search engine optimization?   240
       Meta description   240
       Valid HTML   241
       Keywords   244
       Links   244
    Launching our website   244
       Buying a domain name   244
    Google analytics   250
       Google Search Console   253

Summary 254
Chapter 11: What is Bootstrap? 255
  What is Bootstrap? 255
    Components 259
    Bootstrap Grid system 263
    Media queries 266
  Summary 267
Chapter 12: Building a Website with Bootstrap 269
  Installing Bootstrap 270
    Setting up our project 271
  Bootstrap navbar 273
    Coding the Bootstrap navigation 275
    Styling our navigation bar 280
    Styling the hero section 284
  Styling the Blog section 287
  Styling the about section 295
  Styling the partner section 298
  Styling the footer 299
  Summary 303
Chapter 13: Introduction to Client-Side Rendering 305
  What is server-side rendering? 305
  What is client-side rendering? 306
  Pros and cons of server and client-side rendering 306
    Server-side rendering 307
    Client-side rendering 307
  Introducing to VueJS 307
    Setting up VueJS 309
  Creating a weather application in VueJS 314
    Vue Material 315
    Components 317
    OpenWeather API 318
    The API call 322
  Summary 327
Chapter 14: Tools to Help Your Workflow 329
  HTML Boilerplate 330
  Lorem Ipsum 331
  CSS preprocessor – LESS 332
  CSS preprocessor – SCSS 333
  ColorZilla 334
  Foundation 335
  Fontastic 336

webflow   337
Modernizr   338
CSS3 Generator   338
git   339
CodeKit   341
Animate.css   342
TinyPNG   343
Unsplash   344
Summary   344

Other Books You May Enjoy   345

Index   349

Preface

I'm still amazed when I see how the web has evolved since I started working in this field. I have always liked the fact that the internet is a fast-moving technology—technology, design, process, and everything changes so quickly.

Practical Web Design is a complete hands-on book of Web designer. Every chapter has been thoroughly revised to deliver information, tips, and approaches that are easy to understand and simple to use.

The first part of this book is about the fundamentals of web design. It focuses on its history, evolution, and also the principal components. We will finish this book with a step-by-step design workflow and a comparison between Responsive design and Adaptive design.

The second part of this book will teach you how to build and implement your website from scratch, with an introduction to Bootstrap framework, client-side rendering, and the best tools for your design workflow.

Who this book is for

Practical web design teaches readers the fundamentals of web design and how to build a Responsive website with interaction and dynamic content from scratch. It's the perfect book for anyone who wants to learn web design and frontend development. It's suitable for people with no experience but also great for anyone with some experience and are willing to improve it.

What this book covers

Chapter 1, *Evolution of Web Design*, is about the history of web design, from the beginning of the web with Sir Tim Berners-Lee, how the World Wide Web started, to its evolution now.

Chapter 2, *Web Design and its Components*, is about components in web design. This book will help you understand each component, their usage, and why it's useful in your design.

Chapter 3, *Website Designing Workflow*, is about web design workflow. This book will go through all the processes from start to launch, from concept to launch, step by step.

Chapter 4, *Responsive Versus Adaptive Design*, compares the Responsive design and Adaptive design. It will show you which process will suit your project best.

Chapter 5, *Learning HTML5*, teaches you the basic of HTML5, how to build and structure an HTML page.

Chapter 6, *Learning CSS3*, helps you to understand the fundamentals of CSS, how to stylize your HTML page with CSS.

Chapter 7, *Building Your Own Website*, goes through all the processes of building a website and introduces the HTML Boilerplate and help you step your project correctly.

Chapter 8, *Making Our Website Responsive*, shows you step by step how to make your website Responsive with an introduction to jQuery.

Chapter 9, *Adding Interaction and Dynamic Content*, add interaction and dynamic content to your website and teaches you how to call an API and show information on your website.

Chapter 10, *Optimizing and Launching Our Website*, teaches you how to optimize your website using different tools and analytics.

Chapter 11, *What is Bootstrap?*, explores all the possibilities with Bootstrap Framework, including Bootstrap Grid System, buttons, and forms.

Chapter 12, *Building a Website with Bootstrap*, builds a website with Bootstrap Framework and helps you understand the difference and the advantage of it.

Chapter 13, *Introduction to Client-Side Rendering*, introduces you the world of client-side rendering, with a quick example of a Weather Project.

Chapter 14, *Tools to Help Your Workflow*, lists the best tools to enhance your design workflow.

To get the most out of this book

To get the most out of this book, it's best to have a bit of design experience, but it's not necessary. You can go through this course without any knowledge whatsoever.

Furthermore, you'll need a computer running on Windows, or OS X; the latest version of your favorite internet browser (Chrome, Firefox, or Safari); and a code editor, in this book, we'll use Atom.

Download the example code files

You can download the example code files for this book from your account at `www.packtpub.com`. If you purchased this book elsewhere, you can visit `www.packtpub.com/support` and register to have the files emailed directly to you.

You can download the code files by following these steps:

1. Log in or register at `www.packtpub.com`.
2. Select the **SUPPORT** tab.
3. Click on **Code Downloads & Errata**.
4. Enter the name of the book in the **Search** box and follow the onscreen instructions.

Once the file is downloaded, please make sure that you unzip or extract the folder using the latest version of:

- WinRAR/7-Zip for Windows
- Zipeg/iZip/UnRarX for Mac
- 7-Zip/PeaZip for Linux

The code bundle for the book is also hosted on GitHub at `https://github.com/PacktPublishing/Practical-Web-Design`. In case there's an update to the code, it will be updated on the existing GitHub repository.

We also have other code bundles from our rich catalog of books and videos available at `https://github.com/PacktPublishing/`. Check them out!

Download the color images

We also provide a PDF file that has color images of the screenshots/diagrams used in this book. You can download it here: `https://www.packtpub.com/sites/default/files/downloads/PracticalWebDesign_ColorImages.pdf`.

Conventions used

There are a number of text conventions used throughout this book.

`CodeInText`: Indicates code words in text, database table names, folder names, filenames, file extensions, pathnames, dummy URLs, user input, and Twitter handles. Here is an example: "Let's create this folder and call it `Racing Club Website`."

A block of code is set as follows:

```
<html> <!--This is our HTML main tag-->
 <head> <!--This is our head tag where we put our title and script and all
infos relative to our page.-->
  <title>My Page Title</title>
 </head>
 <body> <!--This is where all our content will go-->
  <h1>John Doe</h1>

 </body>
</html>
```

When we wish to draw your attention to a particular part of a code block, the relevant lines or items are set in bold:

```
.content {
  background-color: red;
  width: 75%;
}
.sidebar {
  background-color: green;
  width: 25%;
}
```

Bold: Indicates a new term, an important word, or words that you see onscreen. For example, words in menus or dialog boxes appear in the text like this. Here is an example: "then click on the three dots at the right-hand corner and click on **Show device frame**."

Warnings or important notes appear like this.

 Tips and tricks appear like this.

Get in touch

Feedback from our readers is always welcome.

General feedback: Email feedback@packtpub.com and mention the book title in the subject of your message. If you have questions about any aspect of this book, please email us at questions@packtpub.com.

Errata: Although we have taken every care to ensure the accuracy of our content, mistakes do happen. If you have found a mistake in this book, we would be grateful if you would report this to us. Please visit www.packtpub.com/submit-errata, selecting your book, clicking on the Errata Submission Form link, and entering the details.

Piracy: If you come across any illegal copies of our works in any form on the Internet, we would be grateful if you would provide us with the location address or website name. Please contact us at copyright@packtpub.com with a link to the material.

If you are interested in becoming an author: If there is a topic that you have expertise in and you are interested in either writing or contributing to a book, please visit authors.packtpub.com.

Reviews

Please leave a review. Once you have read and used this book, why not leave a review on the site that you purchased it from? Potential readers can then see and use your unbiased opinion to make purchase decisions, we at Packt can understand what you think about our products, and our authors can see your feedback on their book. Thank you!

For more information about Packt, please visit packtpub.com.

Evolution of Web Design 1

I still remember back when I was a kid, I used to browse the internet with my 56k modem. It seemed terrific at the time! Websites were loading very slowly, but they were designed to minimize the consumption of data we were using since each kbit was calculated as usage (no unlimited internet, ha!). To understand how web design works, I strongly think that we need to know the history behind it, how developers and designers were designing websites when it first started in 1991 with Tim Berners-Lee's first website. The evolution of web design with table-based sites, animated text and GIF images, free page builders, and the introduction of Flash by Macromedia in 1996 was a significant advancement in the world of web design. It will really help you understand the web design principles of why and where it was heading. Let's go through these key aspects to have a precise idea of how web design has evolved and to analyze its importance in our day-to-day life in contemporary society.

In this chapter, we will cover the following:

- The first ever website: *The beginning of the World Wide Web*
- Table-based layouts: *Introducing table markup in HTML*
- Introduction of Flash: *The renaissance of web design*
- CSS—the savior: *A new way of designing websites*
- Web 2.0: *JavaScript—A new intelligence for web*
- The rise of the mobile: *The boom of mobile web design*
- Responsive web design: *Designing for mobile and desktop*
- Flat design: *The rise of a new design trend*

The first ever website

The first ever website was created by a scientist named Sir Tim Berners-Lee in 1990. He was a British computer scientist at CERN, the European Organization for Nuclear Research. It was basically a text-based website with a few links. A copy of the original page from 1992 still exists online. It simply existed to serve and tell people what the **World Wide Web (WWW)** was:

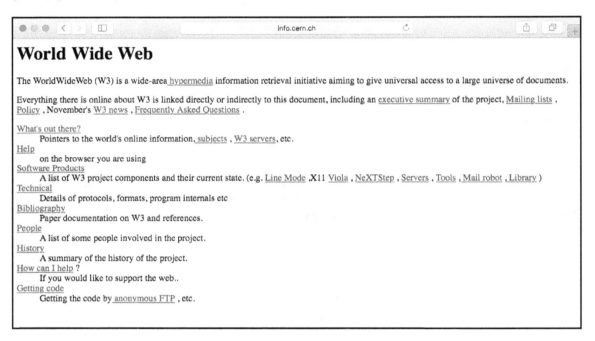

Most websites to follow were pretty much the same. There were entirely text-based with simple HTML markup:

- `<h1>` for titles
- `<p>` for paragraphs
- `<a>` for links (we will go through all this markup in our HTML course)

The following version of HTML further allowed people to insert images, `<img>`, and tables, `<table>`, thus creating more possibilities.

In 1994, the WWW Consortium (W3C) was formed to set and establish the standard of the web (`https://www.w3.org/`). It was mainly to discourage and prevent private companies from building their own web language, as it would create chaos on the web. The W3C to this day continues to deliver standards for the open web, such as the new HTML5 or CSS3.

Here are some examples of websites in the 90s. The following screenshot shows how the Yahoo web page used to look back in 1994:

The following screenshot shows how the Google web page used to look back in 1996:

Table-based layouts

Web design became more interesting with the introduction of table markups in HTML. Web designers saw the opportunity to structure their design with the original table markup (sneaky as they always are). Sites were still text heavy, but at least they could separate the content into different columns, rows, and other navigation elements. The usage of spacer GIFs, introduced in David's Siegel's book *Creating Killer Sites* in 1996, allowed web designers to play with white space (basically, small transparent GIFs were placed in between the content), and by incorporating a sliced image background, users would have an illusion of a simple structure, whereas in reality there was a table layout behind it. Designers could finally play around with some graphic design elements as it grew rapidly in popularity, such as having visit counters, animated GIFs, and so on. Texts and images were literally dancing across websites everywhere.

We can see this in this website from 3drealms in 1996, which shows all the fancy elements designers used to add to their websites:

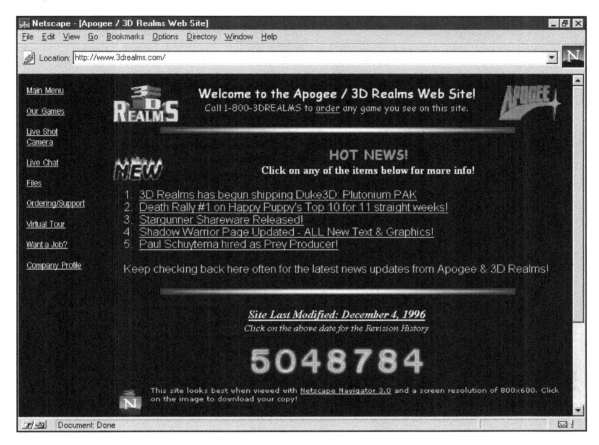

We can also see the evolution of the Yahoo web page in 2002:

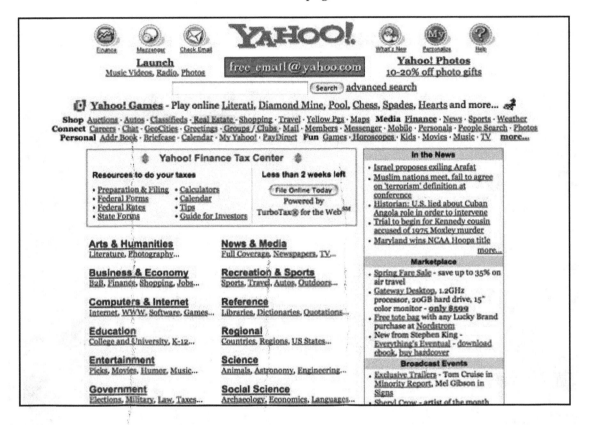

Introduction of Flash

Flash, previously Macromedia Flash and currently Adobe Flash, was created in 1996. It was like a renaissance for web design. People would probably make fun of you if you built your website with Flash today, but back then it was the killer tool to create interactive and graphics websites. Designers were able to add animation, custom fonts and shapes, 3D buttons, splash pages, and all in one tool-Flash. The whole was encapsulated into one file to be read into the user's browser. It was like magic. Unfortunately, that magic was inconvenient. It was not **Search Engine Optimization** (SEO)-friendly and was very heavy in terms of resources for your computer.

Flash started to decline when Apple decided to stop supporting Flash in their iOS software back in 2010 (`https://www.apple.com/hotnews/thoughts-on-flash/`). With the new features of HTML5/CSS3, where you are able to create animation and add multimedia content, designers and developers soon diverted from Flash, at least for web design.

Here are some examples of Flash websites. This screenshot shows a very basic flash website that uses sliders, animations, and interactions. You can check this website at `http://www.richard-goodwin.com/flash/indexn.html`.

Here's one impressive Flash website that was around when I started web design, *Immersive Garden*:

CSS – the savior

Cascading Style Sheets (**CSS**) became more popular in the 2000s with their increasing support in web browsers. CSS defines how the HTML is displayed, and this has allowed designers to separate the content and the design, making websites easier to maintain and quicker to load. You could change the entire look of a CSS-based website without touching the content.

CSS really made the difference as an alternative to Flash. Recommended by the W3C as a best practice, it provides a cleaner semantic, resulting in better SEO.

However, one downside of CSS was the lack of support from various browsers: one browser would support the newest feature, while another would not. It was a nightmare for developers.

We'll look into this with further details in `Chapter 6`, *Building Your Own Website*, of the book. Here are some design changes in Yahoo's website (2009):

Web 2.0

The early 2000s saw the rise of JavaScript. This is when things really started to move towards the web we know today. JavaScript was the first means of adding intelligence to the web. Designers were able to add interaction, complex navigation, and multimedia applications to their design.

While the very beginning of the web seemed to focus mainly on design and aesthetics, it soon, however, became user-centered with usability as the main focus. Designers were also more aware of color distribution, placements, attention to typography, and the usage of icons instead of text links. At last, the evolution of Web 2.0 also saw the growth of SEO, as content driving. These techniques, such as keyword optimization, tagging, and inbound and outbound links, are still being used now. The web industry really saw the importance of SEO, and this became the main focus of web design during this time.

Here are some examples of websites:

We can see the difference in terms of the design. The layout and content are more structured. With *MySpace* website, developers started to create applications for people to interact with:

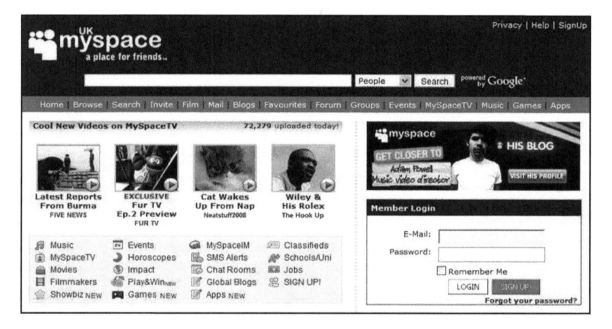

The rise of the mobile

I still remember when the first iPhone came out. It was pretty clear to me that I would not buy one. I clearly didn't know myself at the time. The iPhone ultimately started the boom of mobile browsing. Nobody in the web industry saw this coming; how could users browse a website on a screen so small? It was clearly not user-friendly at all. Web designers started to design a second website that would show only on mobile. I still remember those links started with `m.domainname.com`. It was definitely a hassle to maintain two websites. People were starting to access websites from their mobile more and more.

In 2016, for the first time in the world, mobile and tablet internet usage exceeded desktop usage:

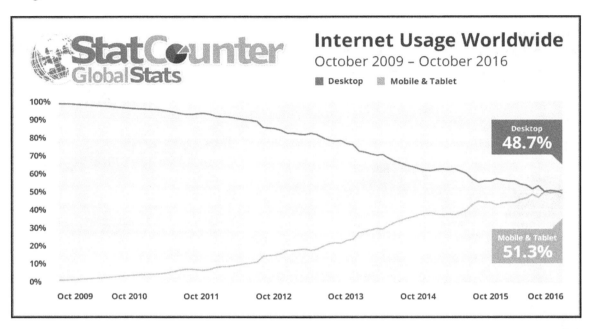

StatCounter Stats http://gs.statcounter.com/press/mobile-and-tablet-internet-usage-exceeds-desktop-for-first-time-worldwide

Responsive web design

The first time we heard the term *responsive web design*, it was from Ethan Marcotte in 2011. In his book on responsive design, he described a new way of designing for the desktop but also for the mobile interface, basically proposing to use the same content, but a different layout for the design on each screen. The introduction of the 960 grid system also helped this responsive issue (`https://960.gs`). The most popular versions being used were either 12 or 16 columns. It became a standard for designers to design their websites using 12 columns for desktop and downgrading progressively for mobile viewing. With the introduction of **media queries** with CSS3, it became easier for designers to design websites for mobile screens.

We will be exploring this subject in further detail in the next chapter.

Media queries is a CSS3 module allowing content rendering to adapt to conditions such as screen resolution (for example, a smartphone screen compared to a computer screen). From left to right, we have the iPhone, iPad, and desktop version. This is a perfect example of a grid system and media queries (`https://www.wired.com/2011/09/the-boston-globe-embraces-responsive-design/`):

Flat design

You've probably heard of this term. If not, flat design is the term given to the style of design in which elements do not have stylistic shapes and characters, such as gradient, drop shadows, textures, and any type of design that makes it look real and three dimensional. It's usually described as the opposite of *rich design*, which in contrast is used to make elements feel more tactile, real, and usable for users when they're navigating.

People often say that flat design originated from the Swiss Style. If you haven't heard of this, Swiss Style (also known as International Typographic Style) was the dominant design style back in the 1940-50s and started in Switzerland:

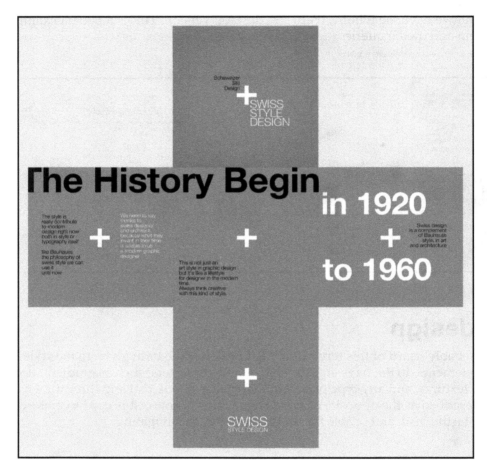

It still has a profound influence on graphic design as a part of the Modernist movement in many design-related fields. It became a solid foundation for graphic design in the mid-20th century around the world. The main characteristics of this design style are the use of asymmetric layouts, grids, sans-serif typefaces such as Akzidenz Grotesk, and a clean hierarchy of content. The famous typeface Helvetica was created during this period and was used in every type of design.

We can without a doubt say that the Swiss Style has had a strong influence on the flat design style we know today. However, the main reason for this trend was mainly caused by the development of responsive design during this period, where developers and designers struggled to implement a design that heavily relied on textures, drop-shadows, and background images. Shrinking those patterns for various screen sizes and because of browser compatibility constraints was just too much for designers. They had to go back to basics and simplify their design and make it less texturized. This would result in quicker-loading websites and would be more efficient and easier to design.

Being a designer, I saw this trend on the rise. I still remember designers testing out the latest features of CSS3 and trying to use as few design assets as possible while attempting to create everything by code. The main focus for both developers and designers at this time was efficiency and faster loading.

But the one thing we can agree on is that both Microsoft and Apple have had a major influence and popularized this trend even further. With Microsoft Metro and the launch of iOS 7 by Apple, people immediately felt that the so-called rich design was completely outdated and quickly found the need for a redesign of their website or app.

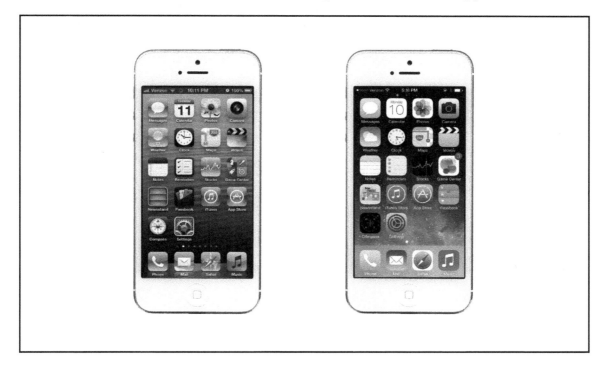

Comparison between iOS 6 and iOS 7

What's next?

After reviewing all these important web design traits, an important thing to remember and keep in mind is that web design trends do not derive from any particular person or company. Web design is a mix of visual design (influenced by print design) and the technology used on the web. With the advancements made in HTML5 and CSS3, we can start to see that design is becoming far more complex as compared to the original flat design. Technology now allows people to have more flexibility with their design and forms. Let's see how the web design trend will evolve, but keep in mind that it evolves quickly, very quickly.

Summary

To summarize this chapter, we saw how the web started with the first ever website by Sir Tim Berners-Lee, and how the web has evolved over the years with table-based layouts, Flash, the CSS, and especially the rise of smartphones, which have changed how users browse the web globally. With this history in mind, we can now jump to the second chapter, which will tackle web components and explain their usage. So, let's get started!

Web Design and its Components

2

In `Chapter 1`, *Evolution of Web Design* we looked at how web design has evolved since the first web page of Sir Tim Berners-Lee in 1990. Throughout those years, we saw new elements and styles emerging in website design. Some elements will help the user navigate through the website, some will help tell a story, but most importantly, all of them have the potential to improve the visitor's experience. In this chapter, I will help you understand each component, its usage, and why it's useful. Let's dive into it!

The following is a list of the components we'll be covering:

- Grids
- Call to Action
- Breadcrumb
- Search bar
- Icons
- Modal
- Typography
- Colors
- Usability
- Consistency

Grids

If you remember, we talked about grids in the first chapter. Grids help a lot with Responsive design, but their use does not stop there. Designers have used grids since print design, for books, publications, and especially magazines. To simply define it, a grid system is a system that helps designers structure their design, content, and imagery, and make it more readable and manageable.

Understanding grids is very important because they will help you design in proportion, balancing between the elements in your design, organizing modules, and sections. And more importantly, it will help the user navigate with the consistency and familiarity of your design grid:

The Grid System

The ultimate resource in grid systems.

About

" The grid system is an aid, not a guarantee. It permits a number of possible uses and each designer can look for a solution appropriate to his personal style. But one must learn how to use the grid; it is an art that requires practice. "
Josef Müller-Brockmann

Unit Grid System

Tools

February 1, 2014

An unitless, fluid, elastic, semantic, responsive, scalable, debuggable, declarative, simple to use grid system. And... HTML5 and CSS3 ready.

Tags: CSS3, framework, grid system, HTML5, responsive

Grid-Based Web Design, Simplified

Articles

February 1, 2014

If you want to reap their benefits of grids on your next project but are unsure of the specifics, this article is for you.

Tags: grid system

Marcus Gärde Grid System

Articles

February 1, 2014

A new method developed by Marcus Gärde to produce grid systems based on old books and scrolls.

Tags: baseline grid, grid system

Grids, Design Guidelines, Broken Rules, and the Streets of New York City

Articles

February 1, 2014

What do the streets of New York City have to do with web and graphic design? For better or worse, the grid.

Tags: efficiency, foundation, grid system

GuideGuide

Tools

February 1, 2014

GuideGuide is a Photoshop extension that allows you to easily create grids with guides.

Tags: grid system, guides, photoshop

Basel;ne

Tools

February 1, 2014

Basel;ne is a typographic experiment focused on vertical rythm and real baseline grid for modern browsers.

Tags: baseline grid, typography, vertical rhythm

The Grid system website (`http://thegridsystem.net/`), is a very useful tool for every grid system, and is a must-know.

The cons

There are always advantages and disadvantages on everything, and the grids don't escape that rule. The first disadvantage of grids for most people and especially those who are new to design is that they may feel the grid system can be a little restrictive and repetitive creatively. Totally understandable and unfortunately, it happens from time to time that you feel like it's difficult to think outside the box and it can feel like you are creating the same thing again and again. But keep in mind that the grid is not easy to take over and needs practice and experience to fully use it to its advantage.

The grids are here to help, but like all rules when designing, rules are made to be broken. You don't necessarily need to stick to the grid, but you do need to understand how it works before breaking the rules. Let's have a look at some good examples of the use of grid layout:

http://kinfold.com

Awesome usage of the grids, elegant, and simple. You can clearly see the composition and the layout. You can check the website at (`http://kinfold.com`) You can see that the top part is not part of the grid, but yet it still flows perfectly with the design:

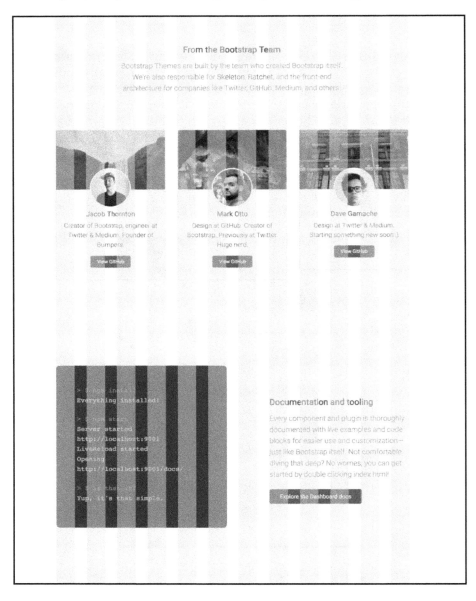

The well-known Bootstrap, a CSS framework based on Grid

A good exercise will be to try to find the grid on a website. And see how it was designed.

Call to Action

A **Call to Action** (CTA) is a marketing term to define a designed element that solicits and encourages an action from the user and which the end goal is to attempt a sale. You'll hear a lot of this term when you start working as a designer when designing websites, especially for marketing purposes. The goal of every designer is to maximize the click conversion on this button, which leads to a sale at the end. Here is some indication of good practice when designing your CTA.

Making it obvious

One piece of advice I'll give is not to be too creative when designing a CTA because it remains a button, and people are used to it. As users have become accustomed to the online experience, they know that CTAs come in the forms of buttons. They see a button; they know what to do. Simple. Make it big, obvious, and stand out from everything around it, and it's in the bag.

Here's an example of a bad CTA:

The area pointed by the arrows are buttons, yes I'm serious, you can click on it. That's why you should keep the CTA as buttons and not as other forms and especially not similar to the content or title.

Using contrasting color

Using a contrasting color allows the button to stand out, drawing the user's eye. The choice of color is also important so be careful of what color you're using. We'll talk about the psychology of colors later in this chapter.

Here's a good example:

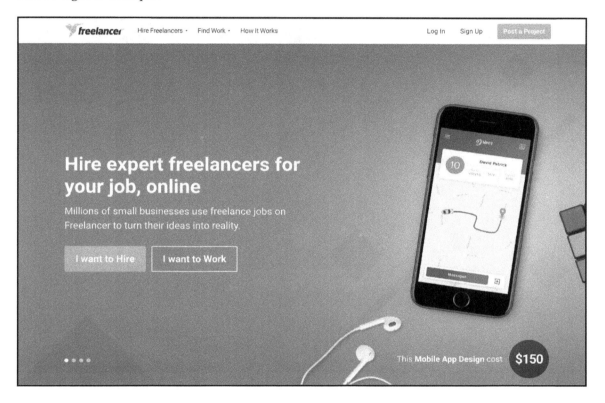

Image from Freelancer.com, all rights reserved to Freelancer International Limited

This example is interesting since the intention here is clearly for the user to focus on the orange button, which the eye will go to naturally. You can catch the user's attention by making your button a contrasting color.

Compelling copy

What you write inside the CTA is also very important. The verbiage should be short. Anything that goes over ten or fifteen words is probably too long. Simple statements are the best.

Here is a good example of good, short, and efficient verbiage:

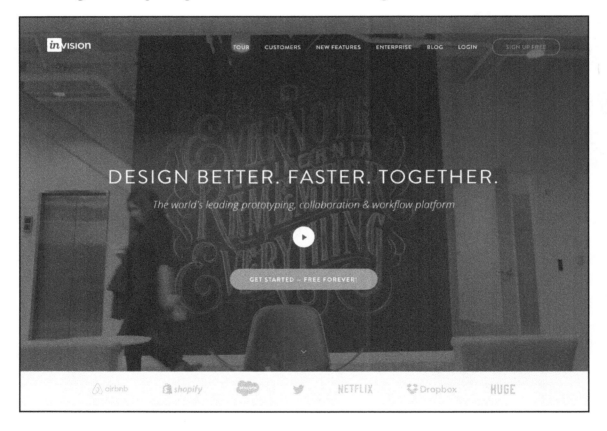

Image from `Invision.com`

Placement

Placement is also very important, and the CTA button needs to be put where the user is going to look next. As a designer, you can anticipate and predict this behavior. You don't need to be fancy, but just logical:

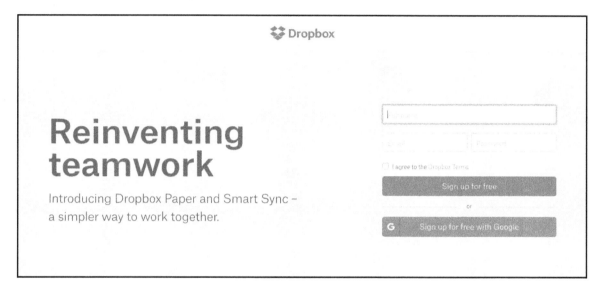

Image from Dropbox.com

Here it's pretty straightforward where you have to click. The CTA is placed logically after the form.

On the other hand, here is an example of something not very straightforward:

Image from Apple.com

In this example, the button is not placed intuitively and the user has to go back up to click on the CTA rather than after the content.

Breadcrumb

Breadcrumb (or breadcrumb trail) is a secondary navigation system that indicates where the user is on a site or web app. The term came from the *Hansel and Gretel* fairy-tale in which the main characters create a trail of breadcrumbs in order to track back to their house. Just like the tale, breadcrumb in web allows the user to find their way back from where they started. It's very useful for complex websites or applications, but not very for a single page website that has no logical hierarchy or grouping.

The following are some examples of breadcrumb.

An example here on Google Drive:

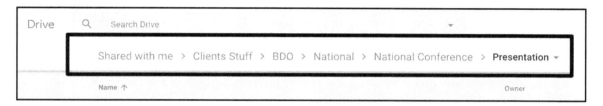

Here's an example of an e-commerce website. (`mac-addict.com.au`):

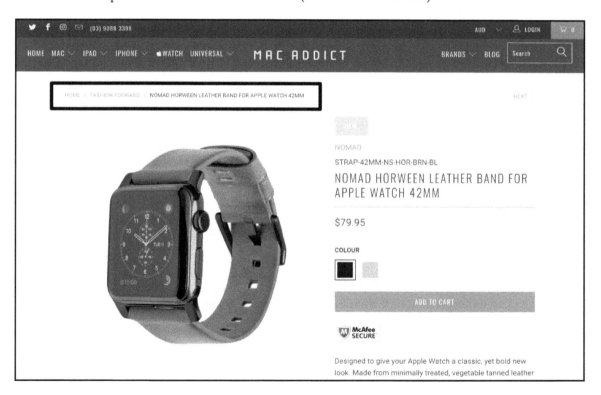

The search bar

The search bar has become more crucial for heavy-content websites, such as YouTube, Facebook, and eBay. Users are now familiar with using a search bar and they're always looking for it when they are searching for something. However, not every website needs a search bar. If you have a simple and intuitive website, light in content, a search bar might be overkill.

The following are some quick tips of good practice when designing a search bar.

The submit button

Designers often denigrate the submit button when designing it, but there is always a reason behind it. Even though users can press the *Enter* button, it's not valuable enough to not display it. Users need to see that there is another action to trigger. It's always better to have different possibilities for your users to achieve their end goal:

Preceding is an example of a bad **Search** bar and a good **Search** bar.

Making it noticeable

It's a bad approach to make the user look for the search box. The search box should always be easy to find, especially when you have a lot of content on your website. Make your search bar stand out by using contrast or color. It's also important to display a full open-text field because a search bar hidden behind an icon makes the search feature less noticeable and increases the number of clicks to access it:

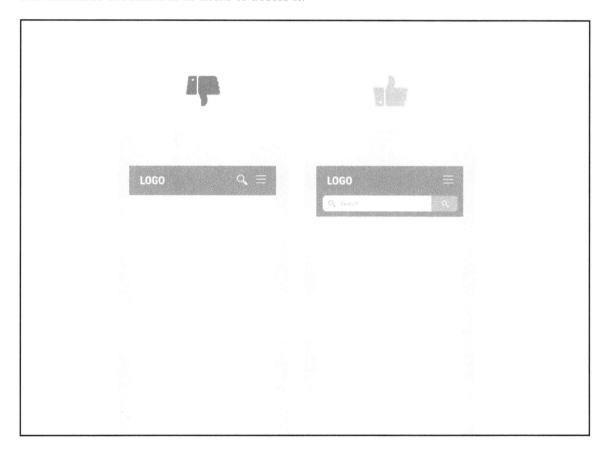

Here's what the Amazon website for mobile looks like:

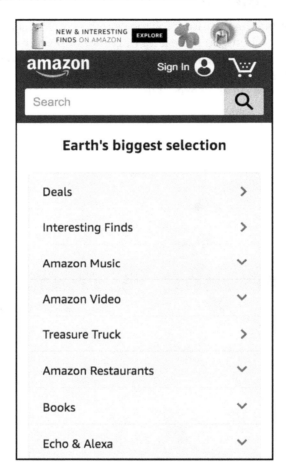

Image from Amazon.com

You can see here that Amazon focuses on this search bar on mobile and doesn't hide it.

Placing the search bar correctly

A search bar needs to stand out, but also needs to be well placed. A study conducted by *A. Dawn Shaikh* and *Keisi Lenz* (*Where's the Search? Re-examining User Expectations of Web Objects*) with 142 participants showed that the most convenient spot for users would be located on the top center or top right of every page on your site.

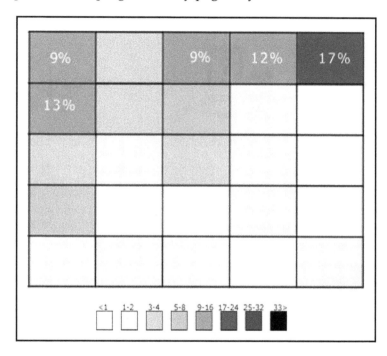

Image from (https://blog.wikimedia.org/2010/06/15/usability-why-did-we-move-the-search-box/)

Icons

Icons are everywhere now, you can find them on road signs, keyboards, interfaces, and so on. Icons help us to better understand and interpret information. It serves as an important visual aid in any graphical communication. As a designer, knowing where and when to use icons to serve your design is really important and crucial. The following are some quick tips to start with.

Describing in a nutshell

It's interesting how icons can quickly summarize what your text is about. Web users have become more proficient at scanning pages for content that is relevant and interesting to them. So by just looking at the icons, they will quickly jump into the information they want. For example, in this example:

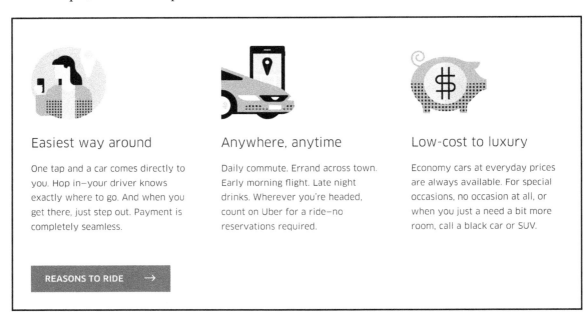

(uber.com)

The icons quickly describe what the content is about with a beautiful effect.

Drawing attention of the users

A website without icons can be quite boring. Imagine a magazine without images, how boring would it be? It's the same logic for icons within websites. Furthermore, with beautiful icons, you are adding more aesthetics to your website, while your users will appreciate you for the convenience:

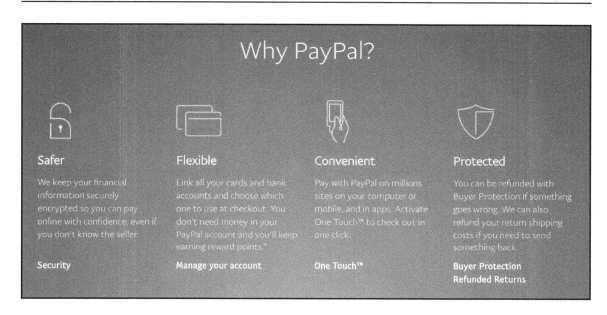

Image from Paypal.com

See this screenshot taken from the PayPal website with icons compared to the following one where we removed the icons:

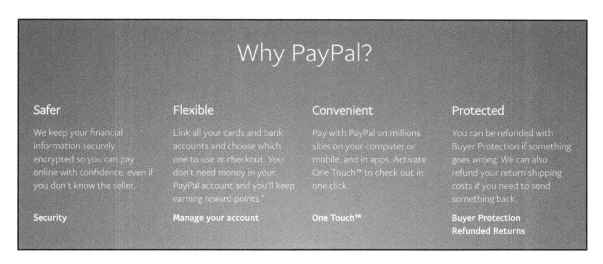

Image from Paypal.com

The first one is definitely more interesting and engaging to read than the second one.

Directional

One of the last reasons I would recommend to use icons is to show the direction to users. Instead of showing *previous* or *next*, showing arrows tends to be even more efficient as users are now used to it:

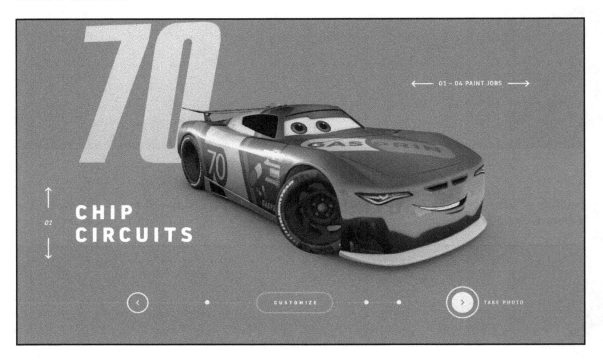

Arrows can be well designed too (http://cars3generations.com/).

Modal

Modal boxes are generally pop-up windows that appear on the screen rather than opening a new tab/window. They usually darken the background to bring attention to the popup. In short, modal boxes are used to show information to the user on the same page without reloading the page and by that, improving the usability.

Modal boxes found their origins from Windows, Mac OSX, and Linux, but they quickly spread out to web applications and other usages.

There are five common usages when using a modal box:

- **Error**: To alert users of an error
- **Warning:** To warn users of potentially harmful situations
- **Collect information:** To collect information from users
- **Confirm or Prompt:** To ask users to confirm an action
- **Helper:** To help users when using the interface

Modal boxes are not to be confounded with modeless components such as sidebars, accordion menus, toolbars, and so on, as they allow users to interact with the parent windows.

The following are some examples of Modal boxes:

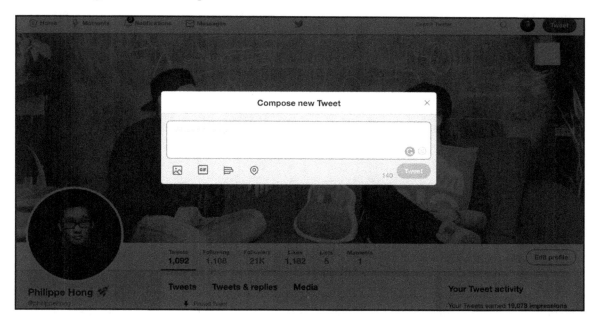

Modal boxes used when composing a tweet on `Twitter.com`:

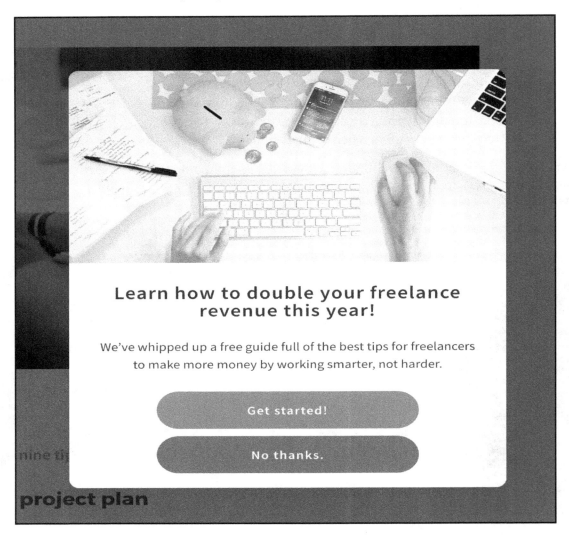

Modal boxes are also used to get people's emails or attention when landing on their website such as the preceding at `Getflywheel.com`.

Typography

I still remember when designing my first website, fonts in web design were very restrictive. A few default fonts were available and we had to stick within most cases with the super neutral **Arial** font. With the font-face roll-out from CSS3, it was now possible to add custom fonts, such a relief for designers! Typography is very important in design, it can alter the perception of your visitors. Using a serif and sans-serif font can literally change the feeling of a website. A study was shown in the *New York Times* (`https://opinionator.blogs.nytimes.com/2012/08/08/hear-all-ye-people-hearken-o-earth/`) comparing fonts by their truthfulness. Take a look at this first graph:

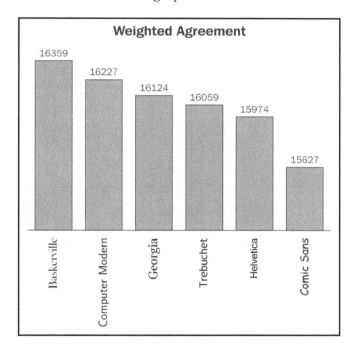

Weighted Agreement

You can see that people tend to believe the information written in Baskerville more than any other fonts:

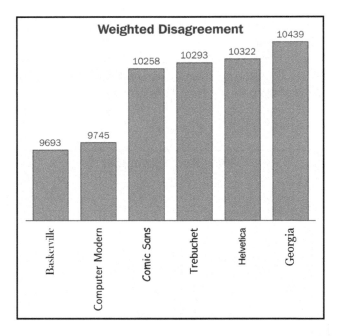

Weighted Disagreement

Typography can really play a role in your design. Unfortunately, I'm not here to do an entire course in typography, but here are some quick tips to choose the best typeface for your design.

Choosing a font that connects your brand

Everything you do should connect to your brand, your typography as well. The typography you choose will give the user an idea of who and what your brand is about. There are essentially three different categories of typefaces: serif, sans-serif, and script.

Serif fonts

A serif typeface is easily recognizable by the little lines or strokes that extend from letters. Here's a figure explaining the difference:

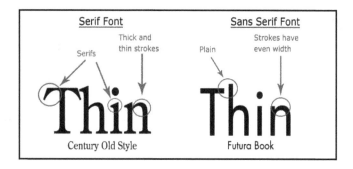

Figure from https://visualhierarchy.co/blog/serif-vs-sans-serif/

The mood associated with serif typefaces is often classic, romantic, elegant, formal, and established. Some famous serif typefaces include Times New Roman, Baskerville, Georgia, and Garamond.

Sans-serif

Sans serif typefaces are often considered more modern than serif typefaces. The mood associated with Sans serif typefaces are more clean, friendly, minimal, or modern. Some of the most famous sans serif typefaces are Arial, Helvetica, Futura, or Gotham.

Gotham Typeface from https://www.typography.com/fonts/gotham/overview/

Gotham Typeface was very popular in the late 2000s.

Casual scripts

These typefaces are designed to suggest informality as if they were written quickly. Many times they appear to have been drawn with a brush. They can represent emotion, speed, and familiarity. They are not great for body content but can act as a very good headline to sell an emotion:

Bellisia font from Creative Market (https://creativemarket.com/sizimon/1719182-Bellisia-Script)

Don't use too much typeface

This advice I always give to young designers because they tend to use too many fonts in their design, too much excitement I guess. Try to be consistent with your design, I would recommend using one to three different typefaces, but no more. Playing with a Serif as a headline and a Sans serif as a body of text is a good pairing.

Here are some examples of good combinations:

A combination of Playfair and Futura (`https://www.dogstudio.co/`)

Another good combination:

Combination of GTWalsheim and Adobe Garamond (`http://www.christianaslund.com/the-new-oil-frontier`)

And lastly, the combination of GT-Sectra and Futura:

Combination of GT-Sectra and Futura (`http://changegout.com/`)

If you want a website to find great combinations of typography, I recommend `https://fontpair.co/`.

There are different ways to add fonts to your website:

- You can either use your own font and use a font generator to generate fonts that are compatible with your browsers. I recommend `https://www.fontsquirrel.com/`.
- You can also use Google fonts, which are free to use: `https://fonts.google.com/`.

Colors

Colors have an enormous importance in web design. According to Kissmetrics, when you view a color, your eyes communicate with a region of the brain known as the hypothalamus, then, in turn, it will send a signal to the pituitary gland and finally to the thyroid gland. This signals the release of hormones that cause fluctuation in mood, emotion, and resulting in behavior. Interesting, isn't it?

Also from Kissmetrics, research has shown that it takes just 90 seconds for a site visitor to form a judgment or opinion. Further to that, 62-90% of that interaction is determined by the color of a product alone.

You should now understand why colors are extremely important and why it's crucial to choose them in the right way, at the right time, with the right audience, and with the right purpose.

What colors mean

Each color draws out a specific emotion in each person. Although, this can differ according to culture, background, or preference. Here is a quick reference of color meanings:

- Yellow:
    - In-your-face yellow should be used with caution
    - Men find it distasteful
    - Kids love it
- Orange:
    - The new red, warm without danger
    - Associated with energy (drinks, sports, fitness)
    - Kids love it too
- Red:
    - Prompts action, increases breathing, and pulse
    - Symbolizes passion and is ideal for fashion/makeup brand, dating, and food

- Purple:
    - Luxury, elegance, and femininity
    - Spans a large female demographic and has no negative associations
- Black:
    - Classy, conventional, corporate
    - Excellence and formality
- Green:
    - Mature, green promotes well-being
    - Ideal for health products, ethical campaigns
    - Lighter greens denote innovation and fresh ideas
- Blue:
    - Popular blue suggests intelligence and serenity
    - Darker blues are associated with luxury products
    - Lighter blues are for refreshing products and ideas
    - Suppresses appetite, so not good for food
- Pink:
    - Good old stereotypical pink
    - Often over-used to attract the attention of female users
    - Anything girly and baby-related
    - It's also known to stimulate the sweet tooth
- White:
    - Pure, cool, calm, and modern
- Brown:
    - Most people avoid this color
    - Disliked by men
    - Evokes nature
    - Denotes dependability

For example, if you want to create an e-commerce website selling toys, you'll not use black because it suggests something more classy and elegant. You will use it more on a luxury brand such as L'Oreal or MAC Makeup:

Image from Loreal.com.

See how L'Oreal uses the black color to look more luxurious even though they are not in the market for luxury.

Of course, remember that these are just guidelines (they always depend on context). Take a look at different websites and see how they use colors, it's always the best way to learn.

Usability

We talked earlier about how design has evolved into a user-centered design. This is exactly what we will be examining now, so what is usability you ask? Usability is simply the attribute that defines how easy the user interface is to use. It's generally measured with five components:

- **Learnability**: How easy is it for the user to achieve basic tasks when landing on the website?

- **Efficiency**: After learning, how efficient is it for the user to redo the tasks or achieve other tasks?
- **Memorability**: How easy is it for the user, after not using the website for a while, to return, and use the website again at proficiency?
- **Error-tolerant**: How easy is it for the user to recover from errors?
- **Satisfaction**: How pleasant and satisfying is it to use the design?

Over the past few years, users have gotten used to certain standards in web design and don't tolerate websites that load slowly, are ugly to look at, or difficult to navigate through anymore. If your website is not usable, there are plenty out there that are. Slow loading speed and bad user experience are some of the factors that can increase the bounce rate of your website. But if you study the needs and the behavior of your users, you'll be able to tailor your content and design according to this. Here are some quick guidelines to give you a preview of what you should be aware of:

Simplicity

Simplicity is definitely one of the things I always aim for throughout my design. Sometimes, a simple CTA in the middle of the page is all you need, not kidding! Try to define at first what your users need, and make the user experience as simple as possible. Adding unnecessary elements that don't serve any functional purposes will inevitably affect the visitors. The famous quote of the architect:

"Less is more"

-Ludwig Mies van der Rohe

is quite accurate to some point.

Navigability

On the continuity of simplicity, having an intuitive navigation is crucial for a good user experience. Don't make the user think. Try to put yourself as the end user and make the navigation as pain-free as possible. Doing some testing with your friends or family is always a good idea.

Here are some quick tips for a good navigation:

- Keep the main navigation simple, somewhere on the top is good.
- Don't forget a navigation in the footer for large websites (people use the footer navigation a lot).
- Include a search box (we discussed earlier as to why).
- Don't make your navigation too complex. Categorize items, but don't go too deep.
- Links should be obvious, underlined, in bold, or in a different color, but they should always stand out from the content.

Accessibility

If your website takes more than three seconds to load, you need to look at optimizing your website. Users nowadays are lazy and impatient. With a world of internet, where everything is fast and easy to access, you need to make your website as accessible as possible.

Here are a few of the basics of availability and accessibility:

- **Uptime**: Make sure that your website is not down or have any errors when loading it. Invest in a good hosting.
- **Broken links**: Make sure that there are no dead links. Users shouldn't land to a 404 page. A good practice is to redirect the user to a new page if the link is unreachable.
- **Website responsiveness**: Make your website available for every screen and support different layouts according to the resolution.

A good example of good accessibility is Amazon. Their website is accessible from anywhere and they have no downtime whatsoever, mainly because they are a hosting company as well. But if you look more closely, their website is responsive in both desktop and tablet, which adapts when resizing. And for mobile, they have an Adaptive website, with a different and cleaner layout, more adapted to a small resolution. We'll see the difference between responsiveness and adaptiveness in one of the following chapters.

Amazon.com on Desktop, iPad, and iPhone

Consistency

After reviewing all these web design components, I'll finish with consistency and why it is important. Consistency is by far one of the key components of a good website. It will bring the last piece of your puzzle for a great website or application. Consider an example of when you want to find your keys, but you know they are always in the same place, you don't have to think. But if you don't find it, you'll start to stress out trying to find it. Websites are the same for users. You don't want them to learn each time they come to your website.

So, how can we be consistent?

These are the few areas that you should be consistent with:

- Design
- Content
- Interaction

Design

Your design should be consistent, which means that every element you create such as links, buttons, inputs, or titles should follow a design identity of your own. Users remember the details whether consciously or not, so they will recognize a link because of its specific colors or shapes.

A **User Interface (UI)** style guide example. This helps to be consistent with your UI:

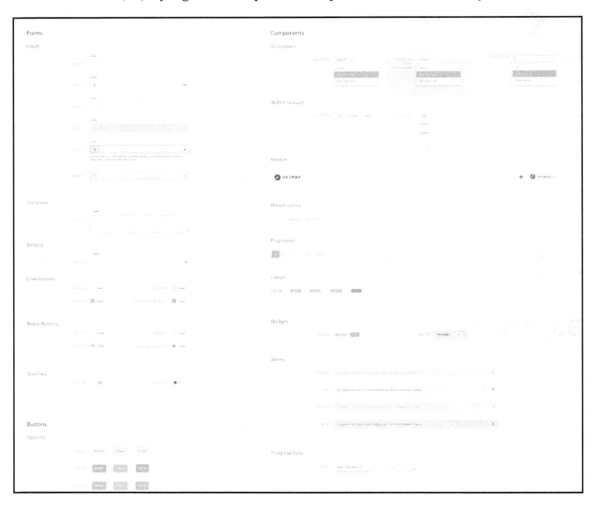

Content

Not only does the visual aspect have to follow consistency, but so does the content. The mood and tone used on the website have to reflect the brand. If you are a corporate website selling to businesses, your website content should both look and feel very professional.

Interactions

Last but not least, interaction has to be consistent throughout the website. How the website is responding to a user's interaction should always be consistent and remain the same. For example, when opening a file on Dropbox, the back button is always situated in the top-left position so that the user doesn't have to look for it again and re-learn your interface.

Summary

In this chapter, we've covered quite a few topics, but to summarize, every component in web design is important on its own, for your design, but most importantly for the end users. With all the tips given, you are now able to create and make a website look great and user-friendly.

Before you start digging into creating your own design, I want to introduce you to the next chapter, which will be talking about Responsive and Adaptive design, something you need to know as a designer or developer. Let's get started!

Website-Designing Workflow 3

Before we really start digging into creating and implementing our first website, I want you to go through all the processes from start to launch. Web design is not just only designing aesthetic websites and beautiful layouts; web design is a whole process, especially when you want to implement your design to the real world afterward.

In this chapter, we'll cover the following:

- Goal identification: *how to identify our goal*
- Scope definition: *List out the scope*
- Wireframe creation: *How to create wireframes*
- Designing: *Framework to create a great design*
- Implementing, testing, and launching

Our situation

Let's imagine yourself working as a designer, and receiving client work. Your first project is to design a website for a Racing Club; here's the brief of the project:

Racing Club is a club for racing fans that was founded in 2016. It started out with a bunch of friends with a love of cars, but it rapidly grew into a community keen to share their passion.

So now, let's go through the entire process.

Goal identification

Within this first stage, you need to identify the website's end goal. By communicating with the client and asking them questions about their business and its goals.

What is the purpose of the website?

This is the right moment to identify the problem to be solved or to set a goal for the website. Sell tickets or increase ticket sales? See what your client wants and find the best solution for it. You also need to do your own investigation, dig into their website, and search for anything that needs to be fixed. With all the fundamentals we studied before, you're now able to see what is good and what is bad.

Who is the website for?

The best way to simplify the design process and the decision making is to know your target audience. There are plenty of ways to know your audience. You can either ask the client, track with different analytics, or check out previous reports on the same market that will help you in that phase.

Is this useful for our audience?

Your client should have some information about their customers, such as their ages, incomes, and so on. Use these pieces of information to create personas, and create user flows that fit the website. In our example, the Racing Club, we would create personas such as the following:

- George: 38 years old, father, garage worker, passionate about racing
- Paul: 28 years old, single, works in finance, has a love for cars and racing

Both users, flows will work differently and you can already suppress any flows that don't concern our target users.

What do they expect to find or do there?

It is also important to know to define the **Information Architecture (IA)** of your website. Knowing what to show your users will set the design of your screens and plan the user experience.

You'll have to create a sitemap and define every screen you need to do. Doing this first will help you greatly in designing your website, as you won't even have to think about it.

Does the website need to follow a brand or have its own brand identity?

Designing a website can be different when you need to follow a brand style guide. As the style guide will help keeping the consistency in the brand, the client will want you to follow it, even if it will restrict your creativity a bit.

If the client doesn't have a brand identity, it's a good opportunity to create one for them.

Are there any competitors? If there are, how is the website different than others?

Knowing a client's competitors is also a good way to know what to do and what not to do. In your process of gathering information, you'll need to research the client's competitors. It's not just about doing something totally different, but doing what is good for the client. If some user experiences of your competitors are good, take inspiration from them, to make your client's website better. You often don't need to re-invent the wheel, but just improve it.

So here's our project.

We need a website with the following:

- Homepage
- Upcoming events page
- Past events page
- Event page details (view info of event and be able to buy a ticket)
- Blog page
- About Us page
- Contact page
- Login page (see the history of ticket purchased)

The website needs to be responsive so people can access it on their mobile. The client doesn't have a brand identity and is willing to let us create one.

The main goal of the website is to firstly show relevant information for the users, and then, if they want, enable them to purchase tickets online instead of going to the physical location.

The following diagram is the sitemap of the website:

Sitemap example

Defining the scope

This is often a tough part for designers: knowing and defining the scope of a project. It's usual for projects to last longer than expected, but this should not be a problem, as it leads to more work. But, sometimes, clients' expectations and your expectations are not the same, so it is best to set boundaries to prevent unexpected work and scope creep. Putting everything in a contract will help you. Here are some templates that you can use: `https://www.smashingmagazine.com/2013/04/legal-guide-contract-samples-for-designers/`.

Creating wireframes

Now that we have defined the goal of the project, we can start designing some wireframes.

In this project example, we'll only do a couple of screens. Here's the wireframe that we'll use for the homepage, events page, and upcoming events page. Wireframes are not meant to be polished and designed, they are just shaped to get an idea of the layout and content. So just use simple rectangles with your favorite design application, or you can even sketch it by hand.

Here's what we came up with:

For the events page:

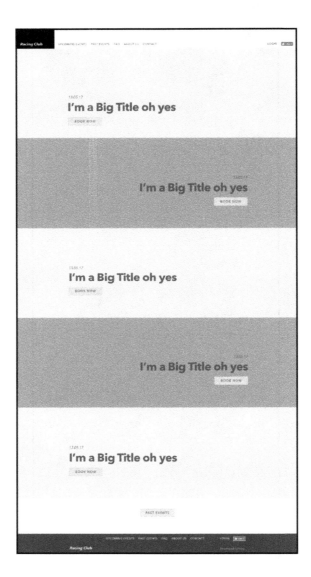

And this is what we came up with for the event page:

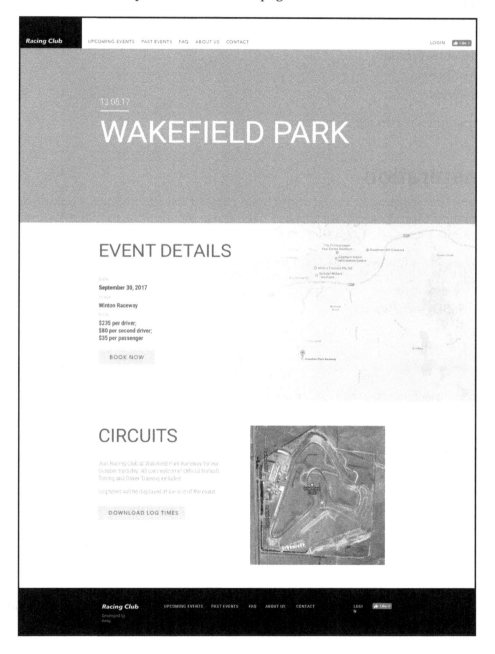

Designing

I always use the same framework when designing a project:

1. Get inspiration
2. Improve
3. Invent

Let me explain what I do for each step:

Get inspiration

I really think that inspiration is one of the main parts of design creation. Looking and gathering inspiration is crucial for me, as I need those inspirations to make my own design by taking a few pieces of design that I'll find cool or relevant for this type of project.

The following are a few websites that I use to find inspiration:

- Awwwards
- CSSDesignawards
- FWA
- Dribbble
- Behance

Then I'll use *BukketApp* to grab images and create a mood board for this specific project.

Improve

Once you have your mood board, you can start to tweak and improve the design. Like a puzzle, try to compose by remixing shapes, colors, and so on. This is the most fun and creative part, because it's up to your imagination and the amount of flexibility you have to create something unique and of high quality.

Invent

When you finally get something from the previous step, you can now expand this design to an entire design style.

This framework can be applied not only in design but in every aspect of a creative or research process. Take a look at biology research, such as biomimetics, which mimics elements and part of nature for the purpose of solving complex human problems. The process is essentially the same, but just in a different way.

Here's the final design that we've come up with:

The homepage design:

Implementing, testing, and launching

With designs approved, it's time to flesh out the design of the pages by implementing the website. It's a very interesting stage, as you will make your design come to life. Seeing and interacting with it will give some interesting feedback that you might not have seen when designing it.

Once everything is done, you'll need to test out each page thoroughly and make sure every link is working. It's also a good way to practice placing your site on a staging website, where people can test it without launching it to the production server. You'll always find issues or mistakes throughout this process. Testing will make sure your website will work perfectly on each browser and each device. It's a long process, but it has to be done!

Finally, everyone's favorite part arrives: the launch is when you see your work finally go out, and you should be proud of it. But, just because you've launched the website, it doesn't mean that the work is over. You can still do some A/B testing to make your design even better, and never forget that a great website isn't just about aesthetics, but finding the right balance between form and function.

These last three steps are part of the next chapters, so we'll go through this process step by step.

Summary

In this chapter, we went through the entire process of designing a website to launch. Understanding the entire process will help you with your clients and your projects. A lot of people rush into their project with design, but there are a lot of steps before the actual design. Especially if you're doing a lot of UX, taking some time by doing some research will actually save you a lot of time and money.

In the next chapter, we'll look into the Responsive and Adaptive designs. The two share similar end goals, yet they are very different. And we'll see how!

4
Responsive Versus Adaptive Design

Before jumping into designing our website, let's understand the difference between Responsive and Adaptive design and why it's necessary to understand it. The differences between Responsive and Adaptive design approaches are very important to know for web and app designers. Knowing these differences will empower you in planning and executing your designs with better vision and results.

With the number of devices we have nowadays, it's important to understand the needs and behavior of each device to really understand how to design it. Content is key, and it needs to flow between each device. See it as water cooling on each device, as Josh Clark says:

> *"Content is like water. Content's going to take many forms, flow into many different containers, many of which we haven't even imagined yet."*
>
> *- (also inspired by Bruce Lee's famous quote)*

Author/Copyright holder: Stéphanie Walter

Designers still get these mixed up and don't really see the boundaries between the two, especially young designers.

In this chapter, we'll learn about:

- Responsive design
- Adaptive design
- Which one is the best?
- And take away from it

Let's get started!

Responsive design

We talked about Responsive design very briefly in `Chapter 1`, *Evolution of Web Design*; if you remember, it describes a new way of designing for the desktop, and also for the mobile interface. It is basically proposing to use the same content, but a different layout for the design on each screen.

To be more precise, a Responsive website shows content based on the browser space. If you open a Responsive website on a desktop and change the size of the browser window, it will dynamically fit the window size and arrange itself.

The concept of Responsive design was first coined by Ethan Marcotte when he wrote an introductory article about the notion of Responsive architectural design, whereby a room/space automatically adjusts to the number of people within it.

"Recently, an emergent discipline called "Responsive architecture" has begun asking how physical spaces can respond to the presence of people passing through them. Through a combination of embedded robotics and tensile materials, architects are experimenting with art installations and wall structures that bend, flex, and expand as crowds approach them. Motion sensors can be paired with climate control systems to adjust a room's temperature and ambient lighting as it fills with people. Companies have already produced "smart-glass technology" that can automatically become opaque when a room's occupants reach a certain density threshold, giving them an additional layer of privacy."

The idea is to have similar behavior in web design. As with Responsive architecture, web design should automatically adjust for users. The ultimate endpoint is to have a seamless experience through every device, and mainly on the client side with CSS (media queries).

To make this easier to understand, look at the following diagram:

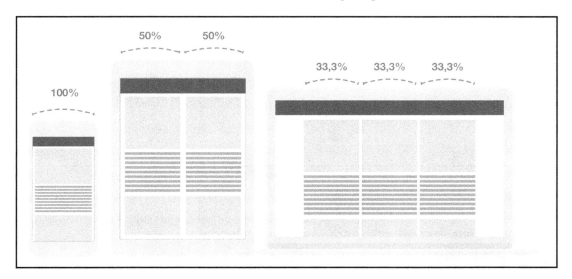

In this figure, you can see the behavior on each device. The desktop view has three columns of 33.3% of the total width. As we go down, we increase this value to 50% and an end to 100% on mobile view. The result, as we can see, is to have content that stretches to fit on every window size, so the content will still be readable on whatever device the user is using.

All the rules are made in the CSS file, so the HTML is not modified whatsoever. This is why CSS media queries are very powerful.

Here are a few examples of good Responsive design:

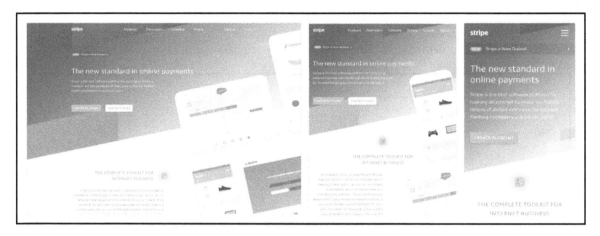

Responsive Layout on Stripe.com

The preceding screenshot from the *Stripe* website shows that the layout is completely fluid and is able to stretch and adapt to various screen resolutions:

Designmodo.com

The preceding screenshot from the *Designmodo* website shows the very clean and clear design that is totally Responsive. You can see that the right sidebar disappeared on both tablet and mobile view.

The *Bloomberg* website

The preceding screenshot shows the *Bloomberg* website. The website is famous for its grid that responds well and lets the users focus on the content.

Adaptive design

While Responsive design works to create a universal look and feel with one design that varies from device to device, an Adaptive design has a different approach. Adaptive design is designed to detect the user device and to redirect the user to a website designed especially for this resolution.

First introduced by Aaron Gustafson in 2011 in his book *Adaptive Web Design: Crafting Rich Experience with Progressive Enhancement*, an Adaptive design has the main difference of having a totally different website on specific resolutions. Resizing the browser has no impact on the design.

The best example of Adaptive design is `Amazon.com`, which displays an entirely new layout of the website on tablet and mobile:

Amazon Website in desktop, tablet and mobile.

If you try to resize your browser, you can see that the design doesn't change any lower than 999 px.

A tool that you can use to test the Responsiveness or Adaptiveness of a website is the inspect tool of Google Chrome. You can just right-click and inspect any element to open the **Developer Console** and click the little icon, as shown in the following screenshot. You can then select any devices from the drop-down on the left.

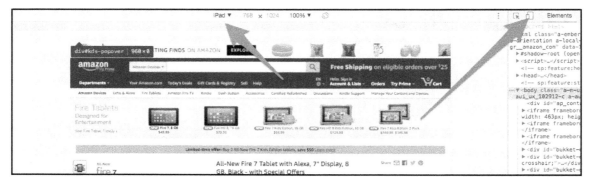

Chrome Inspector with the Device toolbar

So remember that an Adaptive website will not be visible on the desktop, even if you resize it, but only on the device in question.

While Responsive design works on the client-side with CSS, an Adaptive design, on the other hand, works on the server-side. This is really the main difference between the two concepts.

The following are a few other examples:

Opentable.com

The preceding screenshot shows the *OpenTable* website, which has an Adaptive website for iPad view and iPhone view. It's interesting to see how they completely change the layout on mobile view:

Adidas.com

The preceding screenshot from the *Adidas* website shows that *Adidas* has a completely different website on mobile view (`m.adidas.com`), with a more dynamic and user-friendly look:

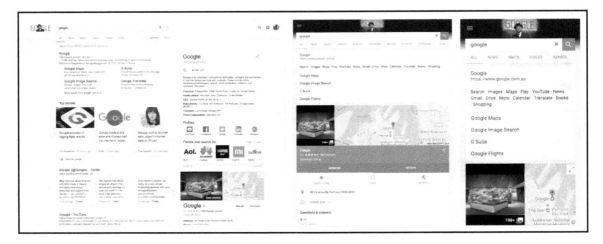

The last example will be Google.com

The preceding screenshot shows the *Google* website. If you haven't noticed, `Google.com` is an Adaptive website when it comes to iPad and iPhone, surprising, no?

So which one is the best?

Responsive design is definitely easier to design and is easier to implement. This is why it's by far the preferred method for creating and designing a website.

However, it will allow less control over the design of each screen. On simple websites, it looks pretty straightforward, but on heavy and complex websites, it tends to be a real headache—components that don't work on mobile (advertisements) or visual hierarchy can become non-user-friendly. Sometimes Responsive websites have an *unfinished* feel, and elements seem to be arranged in a way that just seems to fit the screen, but is not designed for the best user experience. However, there is another approach, which is **mobile first**. This basically starts your design on a mobile and builds up to the desktop. But it still doesn't resolve the problem.

Another advantage of mobile first is speed. Research shows that companies with an Adaptive website will often perform better on loading-speed tests than a Responsive website. This is because Responsive websites usually use the same elements/assets from desktop to mobile, instead of having a specific format and size for mobile websites. However, nowadays, this issue can easily be overcome using media queries, if the Responsive website is properly implemented:

Metric (defaults)	Adaptive	Responsive
Response	568 ms	1,202 ms
Document Complete	1,536 ms	4,086 ms
Webpage Response	2,889 ms	4,860 ms
Bytes Downloaded	2,474,326 kB	4,229,362 kB
Objects Downloaded	20	61

Test carried out by Catchpoint. UXPin (https://www.uxpin.com/studio/blog/Responsive-vs-Adaptive-design-whats-best-choice-designers/).

There are also drawbacks to Adaptive design. Firstly, designing and implementing an Adaptive design is usually a lot more work than designing and implementing a Responsive design. Managing and maintaining two or more different websites requires more infrastructure and budget.

Lastly, while search engines are getting better at recognizing between .com and m.com sites, it's still wise to know that most search engines still don't rank identical content over multiple URLs equally.

The takeaway

Responsive design is the most popular way to design a website cross-devices. It is easier and simpler, but, it can be restrictive in terms of design.

Pros	Cons
Seamless and uniform	Less design control
SEO friendly	Advertisements don't work properly
Easier to implement	Loading takes a bit longer

Adaptive design will be chosen for big infrastructure or complex websites for better control over the design and a better user experience across devices.

Pros	Cons
Allows designers to build a better design and user experience	More work in terms of designing and implementing websites
Designers can optimize advertisements on the device	Challenging for SEO purposes
Loading speed is faster	

There is no good way or bad way to do things. Responsive and Adaptive design are just concepts that are good to understand. You can even use both of them in a single website, using Responsive design for PCs, laptops and tablets, and Adaptive design for mobiles. Just remember this: when it comes to designing websites, the user's needs must always be considered.

Summary

In this chapter, we saw the difference between Responsive and Adaptive design. Knowing the differences will help you when implementing your website.

Now that we have learned the fundamentals of web design, it's time to go on the other side and build your own website. In the next chapter, we're going to learn the basics of HTML and how to build an HTML page from scratch. So, let's dive into coding our first website!

Learning HTML5 **5**

It's finally time to start building our website. First, you'll need to understand the basics of **Hypertext Markup Language** (**HTML**) and CSS. We'll start with HTML with an introduction of what HTML is. Following the structure of an HTML document, we will be filling the structures and will be adding some images and links along the way.

In this chapter, we will cover:

- Atom, our text editor
- HTML tags and attributes
- HTML structure
- Images and links

So, let's get started.

Our main tool

Before we actually start coding, we need to download a text editor. It's a program to basically write all our code. In this course, we will use Atom; you can download the tool via this URL (`https://atom.io/`). The program is available for macOS, Windows, and Linux, and it is completely free!

If you are familiar with another text editor, it's completely fine to use your one. A few other editors are also very nice and free, such as Sublime Text 3 (`https://www.sublimetext.com/`), Bracket (`http://brackets.io/`), and Dreamweaver (`https://www.adobe.com/products/dreamweaver.html`).

Once you have your text editor, we can start the course:

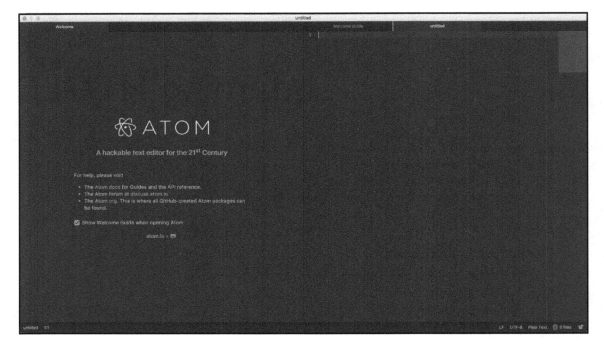

The ATOM Text Editor

First things first, we need to create a folder to put all our project files in there. Let's create this folder and call it `Racing Club Website`. Once you've done that, open this folder as our project folder. Click on **File** | **Add Project Folder...**:

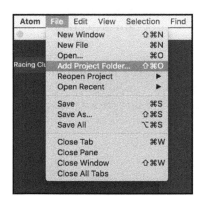

Now that we have our super text editor installed and our project folder set, let's talk about HTML.

What is HTML?

HTML is the standard markup language for creating web pages and web applications. Combined with CSS and JavaScript, you can create simple and complex websites.

Every web page is actually an HTML file. Each HTML file is just a plain-text file, but with a .html file extension instead of .txt.

HTML tags

HTML tags are the hidden keywords that define how you order and display element and content. Most HTML tags have two parts, an opening, and a closing part:

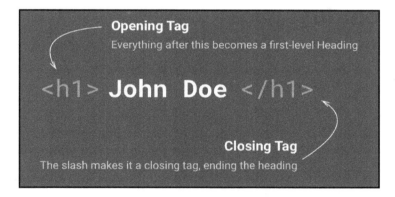

Note that the closing tag has the same text as the opening tag, but has an additional forward-slash (/) character.

There are some exceptions, such as the HTML tag `<img>` that does not have a closing tag:

```
<tagname>Content</tagname>
```

To view an HTML document, you'll need a web browser such as Google Chrome, Mozilla Firefox, Internet Explorer, or Safari.

HTML attributes

Attributes are what customize the tags, and they're defined within the tags, for example:

```
<img src="image.jpg">
```

Attributes are optional for most tags, usually to change the default state of a tag. However, some tags, such as the `<img>` tag, require attributes such as `src` and `alt`, which are needed for the browser to display the image properly.

HTML structure

Every HTML follows a structure so that a browser is able to read the page. To summarize, it always starts with an `<html>` tag. This tag will contain the `<head>` tag and the `<body>`tag. Let's create our first page so you can understand.

Creating our first page

To create our first page. Click on **File** | **New File** or *Command* + *N* (or *Ctrl* + *N* for Windows).

You now have an untitled file. Let's quickly save and name it by clicking **File** | **Save** or *Command* + *S* (or *Ctrl* + *S* for Windows) and name it `index.html`.

Why name it `index.html`? Because the `index.html` page is the common name used for the default page shown on a website by default when a visitor requests the site. In other words, `index.html` is basically the name used for the homepage of the website.

Now that we have our first HTML file, we have to put the essential tags in to make it work. The essential tags should be written as follows:

```
<html>  <!--This is our HTML main tag-->
 <head>  <!--This is our head tag where we put our title and script and all
infos relative to our page.-->
  <title>My Page Title</title>
 </head>
 <body> <!--This is where all our content will go-->

  This is where all my web page content goes!

 </body>
</html>
```

Simply copy and paste the code into your HTML file and open your file with your internet browser (we will pick Google Chrome). Don't forget to save your document!

Your web page should appear as follows:

The web page opened in Google Chrome

Congratulations! You have just created your first web page!

Now let's add some other elements to our page.

HTML elements

There are many different elements in HTML and they are all for different purposes. It's not mandatory to know all of them, but some are essentials for a website. Here are a few essential elements in HTML.

Titles and paragraphs

To insert a title in HTML, there is a tag called <h1> that goes all the way to <h6>. The number is determined by the importance of the title.

Let's put an `<h1>` element into our `<body>`:

```
<html> <!--This is our HTML main tag-->
 <head> <!--This is our head tag where we put our title and script and all
infos relative to our page.-->
  <title>My Page Title</title>
 </head>
 <body> <!--This is where all our content will go-->
  <h1>John Doe</h1>

 </body>
</html>
```

We now have our first title. Let's add a paragraph. To add a paragraph, we can use the HTML tag `<p>`:

```
<h1>John Doe</h1>
  <p>I'm an amazing Designer</p>
```

You learned earlier that for each HTML tag, we have an opening `<tagname>` tag and a closing `</tagname>` tag. This is to basically tell you when your element is ending. You can also add another tag inside a tag. For example, if we want to make some text **bold**.

Let's use our `<p>` tag and add a `<b>` tag to our `amazing` word to make it bold:

```
<p>I'm an <b>amazing</b> Designer</p>
```

This is what you should have in your browser:

John Doe

I'm an **amazing** Designer

This is where all my web page content goes!

Amazing! You just put text in bold! Let's add some forms now.

With forms, no matter what type of information you want from your users, to get it from them you'll need to use the `<input>` tag.

There are many different types of inputs, but, for now, we'll cover `email` and `submit`.

The `input` tag is one of the exceptions that does not need a closing tag; let's add it to our paragraph:

```
<input type="email">
```

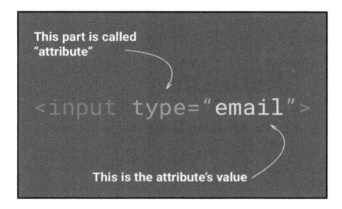

HTML Attribute

You can think of attributes as options for each tag

But the `email` input won't be any good without a **Submit** button! Let's add another input type, `submit`:

```
<input type="submit">
```

Let's see what we have now:

This is what you should have in your browser. Save your HTML document with *Ctrl* (or *Cmd*) + *S* and refresh your browser.

Awesome! But we may have a little problem. We don't actually say what users are supposed to type into the input `email`. Luckily, there is an attribute called `placeholder` that lets us add a default text to our input, so users know what to type:

```
<input type="email" placeholder="Your email">
```

Excellent! Now you can see our placeholder in our email's input.

This is what you should have in your browser. Save your HTML document with *Ctrl* (or *Cmd*) + *S* and refresh your browser.

Links and images

Our last part will be to add images and links.

Web pages will be boring without images. To add an image, you need to add a tag, `<img>`:

img tag structure

You'll need to add the `src` attribute to put the location of your image.

But first, let's create a folder to put all our images inside. Go back to your main folder, `Racing Club Website`, which we created earlier. Inside, let's create a folder named `images`.

In the `Images` folder in code bundle on GitHub, you can see an image called `designer.jpg`; let's copy and paste this image into our folder `images`.

Now that we have the image in your `images` folder, we can link it to our `img` tag. To do so, add the following:

```
<img src="images/designer.jpg">
```

You can put two different types of URL in the `src` attribute. A relative URL, such as the one we put, only works if you're linking to a file on the same domain as the current page. Since we're doing it locally, it's considered the same domain. And an absolute URL, a URL that includes `http://`, directs you to the image directory, for example, `http://philippehong.com/img/image-example.jpg`.

Let's now add a link. Links are added with the tag `<a>` and with attribute `href`.

You can put two different types of URL in the `href` attribute, just as you can for the image. Let's put an absolute URL this time, by adding our Twitter page:

```
<a href="http://twitter.com/philippehong">My Twitter</a>
```

But we still need to add some text inside the `<a>` tag to make it visible.

Your HTML document should look as follows:

```
<html> <!--This is our HTML main tag-->
  <head> <!--This is our head tag where we put our title and script and all
infos relative to our page.-->
    <title>My Page Title</title>
  </head>
  <body> <!--This is where all our content will go-->

    <h1>John Doe</h1>
    <p>I'm an <b>amazing</b> Designer</p>
    <input type="email" placeholder="Your email">
    <input type="submit">
    <img src="images/designer.jpg">
```

```
        <a href="http://twitter.com/philippehong">My Twitter</a>

    </body>
</html>
```

Note that you can see that the code is ready. Let's save our HTML document and see how it looks in our internet browser:

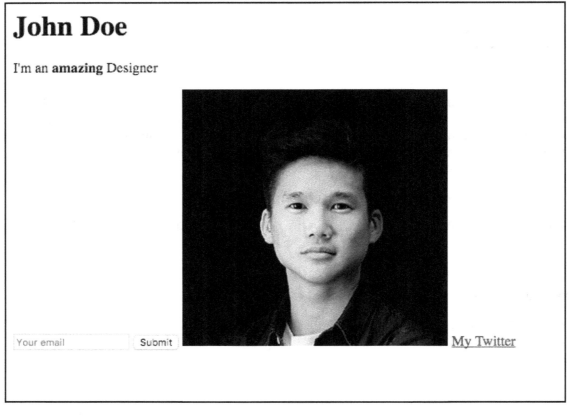

This is what you should have in your browser. Save your HTML document with *Ctrl* (or *Cmd*) + *S* and refresh your browser.

It does look very plain, but this is because we didn't add any CSS.

Summary

In this chapter, we went through all the basics of HTML. We learned about HTML tags, attributes, and also the overall structure of an HTML page.

Before we head over to our next chapter, the tags we learned in this chapter are not the only tags available. There are plenty of tags in HTML, and you can check them out in the glossary at the end of this book. We will also use some new ones when we create our own project! Let's add some styling to our page now!

6
Learning CSS3

Cascading Style Sheet (**CSS**) lets you control the style of the HTML content, change the colors, font, layout, and more. It's fairly easy to understand, and, in this chapter, we're going to tackle the following topics:

- Ways of using CSS
- CSS formatting
- Parent and child elements
- Classes and IDs
- CSS box model
- CSS layout and divider

The different ways to use CSS

There are three ways to use CSS:

- Inside an HTML tag with a `style` attribute (this method is not recommended, but you can still use it a little bit):

```
<p style'"font-size:12px"></p>
```

- Inside our `<head>` section in an HTML document with the tag `<style>`:

```
<style>
  p {
    font-size:12px;
  }
</style>
```

- CSS code can also be put into an external file, linked to the HTML document with the tag `<link>`. The file extension will be saved as a `.css` file:

```
<link rel="stylesheet" href="css/style.css">
```

For this example, we will use the second option, but we'll learn the third option when we start building our own website.

Let's start by adding the `<style>` tag in our `<head>` section:

```
<head> <!--This is our head tag where we put our title and script and all
infos relative to our page.-->
  <title>My Page Title</title>
  <style>
  </style>
</head>
```

CSS formatting

We're now ready to put in our CSS, so how's the formatting in CSS?

CSS is pretty simple to understand:

- **The selector**: This is where you choose which HTML elements you want to add style to. In this example, we select all the `<h1>` elements.
- **Curly bracket**: All styles inside these will apply to the HTML elements chosen by the selector
- **Property**: A property controls one aspect of an HTML element's style, such as text-align, color, width, background, and so on.
- **Value**: The value goes to the property. In this case, the text-align value could be left, right, center, or justify.
- **Semicolon**: It is mandatory to apply it at the end of a property.

You can have multiple styles in the same `<style>` tag. Let's center all the h1 and p tags.

You should have the following:

```
<style>
 h1 {
  text-align: center;
 }
 p {
  text-align: center;
 }
</style>
```

Parent and child elements

What if you want to center all the texts and not just the `<h1>` and `<p>`? There is a simple way to achieve that. You have to understand the parent and child element. Basically, if you style a parent element, all the child elements will have the same styling, unless you specify a specific style for the child element. The following is our example:

```
<body> <!--This is our parent element -->
  <h1>John Doe</h1>
  <p>I'm an <b>amazing</b> Designer</p>
  <input type="email" placeholder="Your email">
  <input type="submit">
  <img src="img/designer.jpg">
  <a href="http://twitter.com/philippehong">My Twitter</a>
</body>
```

The `<body>` tag is the parent of every element that is inside it, which includes the `<h1>`, `<p>`, `<input>`, `<img>`, and `<a>` elements.

Let's remove the previous style and style the `<body>` element with `text-align: center;`:

```
<style>
  body {
    text-align: center;
  }
</style>
```

Let's save the HTML document and reload the page in Chrome. Note that every element has the property `text-align: center;`.

Classes and IDs

We saw how to select HTML tags with CSS, but, most of the time, you'll have multiple identical HTML tags, such as <p> or <a>. How do we differentiate them so we can only select and style a specific one? Here come the classes and IDs. They're used to select a specific HTML tag you have put an attribute id or class, for example:

```
<div id="header"></div>
<p class="big"></p>
```

To select this ID header in CSS, we'll need to write a hash (#) character, followed by the ID of the element, in this case, header:

```
#header {
  margin-left: 10px;
}
```

To select a class, we'll need to write a period (.) character, followed by the name of the class:

```
.big {
  font-size:20px;
}
```

So what is the difference between IDs and classes? The only difference is that IDs can be used only once in an HTML document, while Classes can be used multiple times. We also need to know the following:

For IDs:

- Each element can have only one ID
- Each page can have only one element with that ID

For classes:

- You can use the same class on multiple elements
- You can use multiple classes on the same element

We can, for example, have the following:

```
<div id="header" class="big red blue"></div>
```

Which means that the `<div>` element has an ID `header` and the classes `big`, `red`, and `blue`.

Let's add some classes and IDs into our document now:

```
<body> <!--This is our parent element -->

  <h1 id="my-name">John Doe</h1>
  <p class="text">I'm an <b>amazing</b> Designer</p>
  <input class="form" type="email" placeholder="Your email">
  <input class="button" type="submit">
  <img class="image" src="images/designer.jpg">
  <a class="link" href="http://twitter.com/philippehong">My Twitter</a>

</body>
```

As you can see, I added some really simple IDs and classes so you can understand how it works. We'll go into detail about the best practices when it comes to using IDs and classes.

Now that we have our IDs and classes, let's add some style to our CSS. For that, let's select our first ID, `my-name`, and make it bigger and underlined. For that, we will use the CSS properties `font-size` and `text-decoration`:

```
<style>
  body {
    text-align: center;
  }
  #my-name{
    font-size: 50px;
    text-decoration: underline;
  }
</style>
```

Let's style some classes now. For this example, let's add another `<p>` tag on our HTML document, just before our link, as follows:

```
<body> <!--This is where all our content will go-->

  <h1 id="my-name">John Doe</h1>
  <p class="text">I'm an <b>amazing</b> Designer</p>
  <input class="form" type="email" placeholder="Your email">
  <input class="button" type="submit">
  <img class="image" src="images/designer.jpg">
  <p class="text">Follow me on Twitter</p> <!--Added text-->
  <a class="link" href="http://twitter.com/philippehong">My Twitter</a>

</body>
```

Now that we have two elements with the same class, let's see what happens when we want to style the class `text` by adding a `font-family` property:

```
<style>
  body {
    text-align: center;
  }
  #my-name{
    font-size: 50px;
    text-decoration: underline;
  }
  .text {
    font-family: Arial;
  }
</style>
```

Save your HTML document and refresh your browser. This is what you should see:

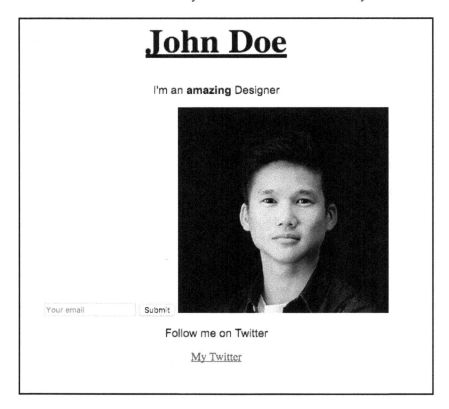

This should change the font of the elements with the class `text`. You can see that both elements have changed.

CSS box model

All HTML elements can be seen as boxes. A CSS box model allows us to define the spaces between elements. Whether you want to add a border, set a margin, or add paddings between elements, you'll need to understand the box model. Understanding this part will help you a lot when implementing your design.

The boxes

The box model consists of four properties:

- **Content**: The text, images, and so on
- **Padding**: A transparent area around the content, inside the box
- **Margin**: The space between the boxes
- **Border**: This goes around the padding and the content

Have a look at following diagram for a better understanding:

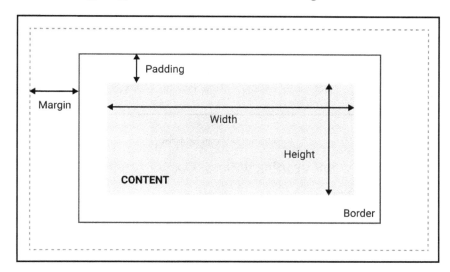

A CSS box model can be described as shown in the preceding diagram.

Box models can also let us set the height and the width of an element. By setting the width or the height of the content with the following:

```
Width: 200px;
```

The width of the content will be 200px.

Now, the annoying thing about the standard box-model is that you can only set the width and the height of the content, and not in the entire box itself, which means the padding, margin, and border will be added to the width and height we specified. Which is quite annoying:

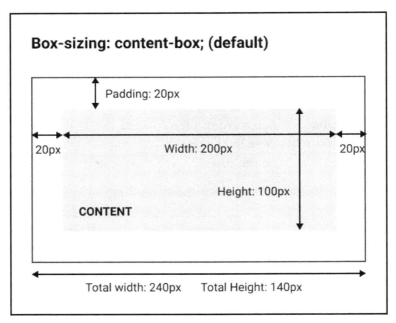

Box Sizing with the property content-box

Fortunately, we can counter this by using the box-sizing property:

```
box-sizing: border-box;
```

By setting `box-sizing` to `border-box`, we will now set the width and height of the entire box:

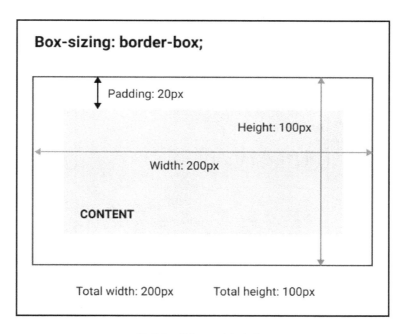

Box Sizing with the property border-box

Block and inline

There is one last thing about box models. In HTML, there is what we call block elements and inline elements.

Block elements: It uses the full width of the browser and always starts on a new line. You can see them as blocks you need to pile one after another. Headings and paragraphs are some examples of block elements.

Examples of block-level elements:

- `<div>`
- `<h1>` – `<h6>`
- `<p>`
- `<form>`

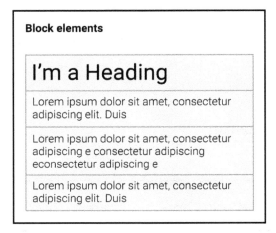

Block elements are represented in red boxes

Inline elements: Inline elements don't start on a new line and only take up as much width as necessary. Look at this example of the blue elements:

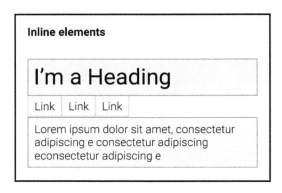

Inline elements are represented in blue boxes

The following are examples of inline elements:

- `<span>`
- `<a>`
- `<img>`

CSS layout and dividers

Now that we understand how the box model works, we can try to build a simple layout for our HTML page, as shown in the following diagram:

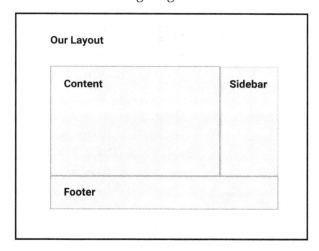

Our layout will have a container with a sidebar on the right, and at the bottom a footer. A very basic layout for a lot of websites.

This layout will be inside a container that will be centered on the page. Without further ado, let's get started!

The basic layout

To create our basic layout, we will use the `<div>` element. The `<div>` element is the most commonly used HTML element. `<div>` stands for divide, and we simply use it to divide our page into sections by creating boxes where we put our contents.

Let's clear our CSS in your `<style>` section and start from scratch.

We'll start first by adding a `<div>` element to wrap all the content we've created, and then add a class `container` to it:

```
<div class="container">
  <h1 id="my-name">John Doe</h1>
  <p class="text">I'm an <b>amazing</b> Designer</p>
  <input class="form" type="email" placeholder="Your email">
  <input class="button" type="submit">
  <img class="image" src="images/designer.jpg">
  <p class="text">Follow me on Twitter</p> <!--Added text-->
  <a class="link" href="http://twitter.com/philippehong">My Twitter</a>
</div>
```

Formatting and indenting your HTML

You can see in my HTML document that my code is indented. Code indentation applies to every language and makes it easier to read and to structure. The basic way of indenting is using the *Tab* key to move the content one step to the right:

This is a basic structure and indentation that you should have.

Styling our class

Let's start by styling on the `container` class that we've just created. For this, let's go to our `<style>` section and add the following:

```
<style>
  .container {
```

```
    width: 960px;
  }
</style>
```

This will set the `width` property to the `<div>` with the class `container` to `960px`.

We want our container to be centered on the page. To do that, we need to add a `margin` property, as follows:

```
<style>
  .container {
    width: 960px;
    margin-left: auto;
    margin-right: auto;
  }
</style>
```

Adding `margin-left: auto;` and `margin-right: auto;` means that the left and right margin are adjusted automatically according to the context of the element, which is the browser window in this case:

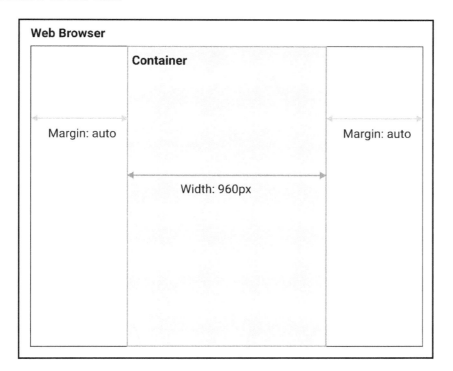

There are a lot of ways to center an element with CSS; this is the first one. We'll check out a couple of other ways in the upcoming chapters.

Now let's create our `content` element as defined in the layout we want to do.

Inside our `<div class = "container">`, let's add our `<div class = "content">`. Again, let's move our content inside this `div`, as follows:

```
<body> <!--This is where all our content will go-->
 <div class="container">
   <div class="content">
     <h1 id="my-name">John Doe</h1>
     <p class="text">I'm an <b>amazing</b> Designer</p>
     <input class="form" type="email" placeholder="Your email">
     <input class="button" type="submit">
     <img class="image" src="images/designer.jpg">
     <p class="text">Follow me on Twitter</p> <!--Added text-->
     <a class="link" href="http://twitter.com/philippehong">My Twitter</a>
   </div>
 </div>
</body>
```

Next, let's add our `sidebar`. After our `<div class= "content">`, add a `div` with the class `sidebar`.

Inside our `sidebar`, add a `<p>` element to create some content:

```
<div class="sidebar">
    <p>Lorem ipsum dolor sit amet, consectetur adipiscing elit. Duis turpis
neque, volutpat ac consequat sed, ullamcorper at dolor. Donec placerat a mi
quis ultricies. Etiam egestas semper tempor. Suspendisse nec eros porta,
rhoncus tortor sed, consequat arcu. Suspendisse potenti. Nunc blandit nisl
eu justo feugiat vestibulum. Vivamus consequat, quam vitae sagittis
maximus, magna lacus fringilla justo, sit amet auctor mi nulla quis ante.
Morbi malesuada gravida turpis, vel lobortis libero placerat sit amet.
Vestibulum sollicitudin semper est eget ultricies. Donec posuere turpis
urna.
   </p>
</div>
```

You can find some dummy text by going to the website `https://www.lipsum.com/`.

Lastly, let's add our `footer` element after our `sidebar` element:

```
<div class="footer">
  <p>This is my footer</p>
</div>
```

Our HTML document should now look as follows:

```
<html> <!--This is our HTML main tag-->
 <head> <!--This is our head tag where we put our title and script and all
infos relative to our page.-->
  <title>My Page Title</title>
  <style>
    .container {
      width: 960px;
      margin-left: auto;
      margin-right: auto;
    }
  </style>
 </head>
 <body> <!--This is where all our content will go-->
   <div class="container">
     <div class="content">
       <h1 id="my-name">John Doe</h1>
       <p class="text">I'm an <b>amazing</b> Designer</p>
       <input class="form" type="email" placeholder="Your email">
       <input class="button" type="submit">
       <img class="image" src="images/designer.jpg">
       <p class="text">Follow me on Twitter</p> <!--Added text-->
       <a class="link" href="http://twitter.com/philippehong">My
Twitter</a>
     </div>
     <div class="sidebar">
       <p>Lorem ipsum dolor sit amet, consectetur adipiscing elit. Duis
turpis neque, volutpat ac consequat sed, ullamcorper at dolor. Donec
placerat a mi quis ultricies. Etiam egestas semper tempor. Suspendisse nec
eros porta, rhoncus tortor sed, consequat arcu. Suspendisse potenti. Nunc
blandit nisl eu justo feugiat vestibulum. Vivamus consequat, quam vitae
sagittis maximus, magna lacus fringilla justo, sit amet auctor mi nulla
quis ante. Morbi malesuada gravida turpis, vel lobortis libero placerat sit
amet. Vestibulum sollicitudin semper est eget ultricies. Donec posuere
turpis urna.</p>
```

```
      </div>
      <div class="footer">
        <p>This is my footer</p>
      </div>
    </div>
  </body>
</html>
```

Now, for the purpose of this lesson, let's add some background color to each element to see how the layouts work. To do this, let's go to our style section and add a background-color property for each class, as follows:

```
<style>
  .container {
    width: 960px;
    margin-left: auto;
    margin-right: auto;
  }
  .content {
    background-color: red;
  }
  .sidebar {
    background-color: green;
  }
  .footer {
    background-color: blue;
  }
</style>
```

Now we will save our HTML document and refresh our browser to see how it looks:

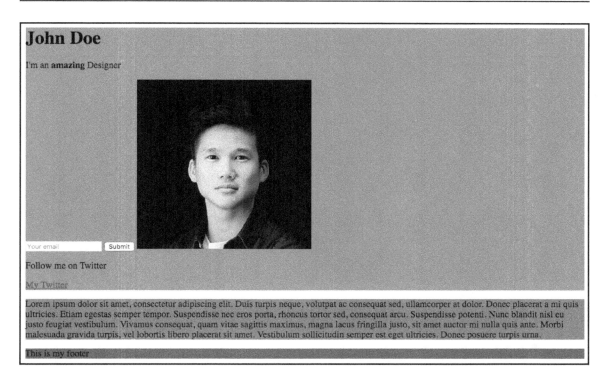

Our web page is pretty ugly, but it does show how the layout is put together. Let's add a few more CSS properties to make it look the way we want it to look.

We want the .content element to be 75% of the total width (960px), and the sidebar to be 25%. We could do some maths and calculate 75% of 960, but, in CSS, you can also set the width by percentages:

```
.content {
  background-color: red;
  width: 75%;
}
.sidebar {
  background-color: green;
  width: 25%;
}
```

Now we will save our HTML document and refresh our browser to see how it looks:

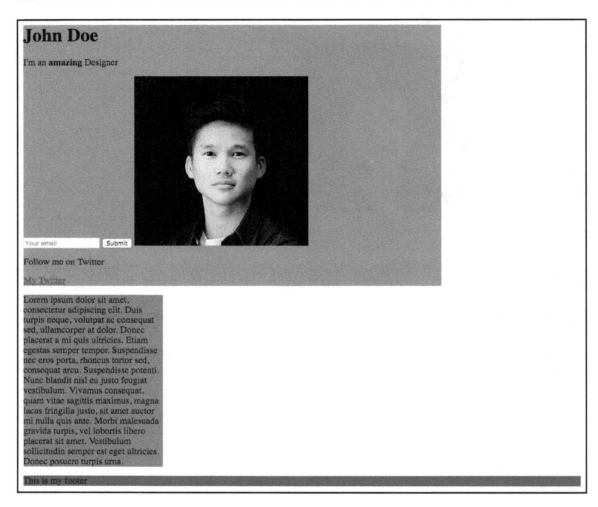

As you can see, our elements have their width properties of 75% and 25%. Now to move our sidebar next to the content, we'll need to use the CSS property called float. With float, an element can be pushed to the left or to the right, allowing other elements to wrap around it. So let's do that:

```
.content {
  background-color: red;
  width: 75%;
  float: left;
```

```
}
.sidebar {
  background-color: green;
  width: 25%;
  float: right;
}
```

Let's save our HTML document and refresh our browser to see how it looks:

Our content and `sidebar` are now side by side, but the problem is that our `footer` is on the right side, as it has the property `float` right from the `sidebar`. To avoid this, we need to use the `clear` property, which counterparts the `float` property. We'll set the property to both, which means right and left:

```
.footer {
  background-color: blue;
  clear: both;
}
```

Save and refresh the document.

We now have our layout fully coded with CSS.

Summary

We finally have our layout now. Again, this lesson wasn't about doing something pretty, it was to help you understand how to properly lay out a page with CSS. In the next chapter, we're going to delve deeper into HTML and CSS by creating and styling our website—how exciting!

7
Building Your Own Website

The fun part has finally come. We're going to start implementing our website from A to Z. I will explain thoroughly through each step. Here's the list of what is going to be covered in this chapter:

- Installation of HTML Boilerplate
- Setting up our project with images, fonts, and normalize.css
- Creating our header and stylising it
- Creating our hero section and learn about the positioning in CSS
- Creating our Blog section
- Adding an about section
- Creating a Partner section
- Creating a footer section

First, let's see the design we're going to implement. If you can remember, we saw a little preview back in `Chapter 4`, *Responsive Versus Adaptive Design*.

Our design

Our home page will contain the following:

1. Header: We will learn how to create and stylize a navigation section, with a logo and a menu on the right-hand side.
2. A hero Image: In web design, it describes a front banner image, usually a big image. We'll learn how to create a full-width background image with a big title.
3. A preview of the `Blog` with six `blog` posts: We'll learn how to display three responsive columns with images and content.
4. An **ABOUT US** section: We will learn how to add a gradient to an image.

5. A **PARTNERS** section: We will learn how to center content on the page.

6. A footer: Basically the same thing as the header, but at the bottom.

You can check the image of the home page in full size in the resources files I provided, in `Resources | Screens`. There is also the `Sketch` source file of the project.

I strongly recommend you to install Sketch or Figma if you're not using one of these design tools yet. The Sketch app is commonly used for web design projects and can be downloaded at `http://sketchapp.com`. It has a free trial period of 14 days. Figma is similar to Sketch and can be used without a trial.

This is what our design looks like:

Our home page design

Without further ado, let's get started!

Installing HTML Boilerplate

We're going to start a fresh, so let's create a new file for this project. What I like to do when I start a project is download an HTML Boilerplate. HTML5 Boilerplate is a frontend template, created to help you build fast, robust, and adaptable web apps or sites. You basically download one package, and it contains all the files you need to start a project.

Let's go to `https://html5boilerplate.com/` to download the latest version of the template:

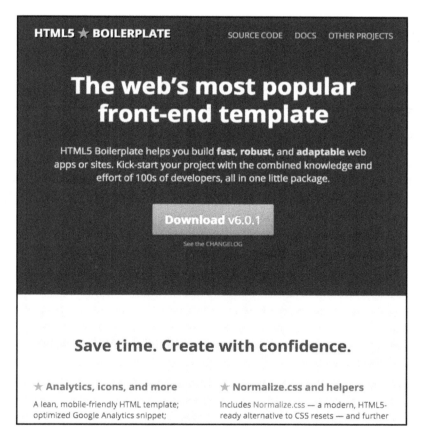

Click on **Download v6.0.1** or higher.

Let's have a look at what's inside our package:

.editorconfig	11 Sep 2017, 5:48 am	191 bytes	Unix e...cutable
.gitattributes	11 Sep 2017, 5:48 am	3 KB	Unix e...cutable
.gitignore	11 Sep 2017, 5:48 am	204 bytes	Unix e...cutable
.htaccess	11 Sep 2017, 5:48 am	40 KB	Unix e...cutable
404.html	11 Sep 2017, 5:48 am	1 KB	HTML
browserconfig.xml	11 Sep 2017, 5:48 am	417 bytes	XML File
▶ css	Today, 4:07 pm	--	Folder
▶ doc	Today, 4:07 pm	--	Folder
favicon.ico	11 Sep 2017, 5:48 am	766 bytes	Windo...n image
humans.txt	11 Sep 2017, 5:48 am	229 bytes	Plain Text
icon.png	11 Sep 2017, 5:48 am	4 KB	PNG image
▶ img	Today, 4:07 pm	--	Folder
index.html	11 Sep 2017, 5:48 am	2 KB	HTML
▶ js	Today, 4:07 pm	--	Folder
LICENSE.txt	11 Sep 2017, 5:48 am	1 KB	Plain Text
robots.txt	11 Sep 2017, 5:48 am	78 bytes	Plain Text
site.webmanifest	11 Sep 2017, 5:48 am	132 bytes	Document
tile-wide.png	11 Sep 2017, 5:48 am	2 KB	PNG image
tile.png	11 Sep 2017, 5:48 am	3 KB	PNG image

There are plenty of files in the folder. What we can see is that it contains all the essential files a website needs to work properly:

- `index.html`: Our home page, the page where the user will land upon going to your website
- The `css` folder: A folder for all our CSS files
- The `img` folder: A folder for all our images
- The `js` folder: A folder for all our JS files
- `favicon.ico`: An icon that shows up at the left corner of a tab of a browser that indicates to the user that they're on your website, usually your logo
- `404.html`: An HTML page for users who landed on an incorrect URL

The rest of the files are not so important for us to understand at the moment; we will review them in an upcoming chapter.

Let's rename our folder to make it our own, for example, `Web Project`.

Editing index.html

Let's now open our folder in Atom; click on **Menu** | **Open...** | and select our Web Project folder.

Select index.html from the left panel. You can see the HTML document and what it contains:

```html
<!doctype html>
<html class="no-js" lang="">
  <head>
      <meta charset="utf-8">
      <meta http-equiv="x-ua-compatible" content="ie=edge">
      <title></title>
      <meta name="description" content="">
      <meta name="viewport" content="width=device-width, initial-scale=1">

      <link rel="manifest" href="site.webmanifest">
      <link rel="apple-touch-icon" href="icon.png">
      <!-- Place favicon.ico in the root directory -->

      <link rel="stylesheet" href="css/normalize.css">
      <link rel="stylesheet" href="css/main.css">
  </head>
  <body>
      <!--[if lte IE 9]>
          <p class="browserupgrade">You are using an
<strong>outdated</strong> browser. Please <a
href="https://browsehappy.com/">upgrade your browser</a> to improve your
experience and security.</p>
      <![endif]-->

      <!-- Add your site or application content here -->
      <p>Hello world! This is HTML5 Boilerplate.</p>
      <script src="js/vendor/modernizr-3.5.0.min.js"></script>
      <script src="https://code.jquery.com/jquery-3.2.1.min.js"
integrity="sha256-hwg4gsxgFZhOsEEamdOYGBf13FyQuiTwlAQgxVSNgt4="
crossorigin="anonymous"></script>
      <script>window.jQuery || document.write('<script
src="js/vendor/jquery-3.2.1.min.js"><\/script>')</script>
      <script src="js/plugins.js"></script>
      <script src="js/main.js"></script>

      <!-- Google Analytics: change UA-XXXXX-Y to be your site's ID. -->
      <script>
          window.ga=function(){ga.q.push(arguments)};ga.q=[];ga.l=+new
Date;
```

```
        ga('create','UA-XXXXX-Y','auto');ga('send','pageview')
    </script>
    <script src="https://www.google-analytics.com/analytics.js" async
defer></script>
  </body>
</html>
```

We'll now review each part of this HTML file so you understand each part of the code:

```
<title></title>
```

Here you will put the title of our website; for this exercise, let's put `Racing Club - Events & Tickets`.

```
<meta name="description" content="">
```

This section is the description of the page, It will be useful for SEO and will appear on a search result after the title.

```
<meta name="viewport" content="width=device-width, initial-scale=1">
```

This will tell the browser how to behave for desktop and mobile view. You can leave it as it is.

```
<link rel="stylesheet" href="css/normalize.css">
<link rel="stylesheet" href="css/main.css">
```

We learned in the previous chapter that there are three different ways to use CSS in our HTML page. We used the second method in our exercise, but the best way to use CSS is to put it into an external file, like so. You can leave it as it is.

```
<!--[if lte IE 9]>
    <p class="browserupgrade">You are using an <strong>outdated</strong>
browser. Please <a href="https://browsehappy.com/">upgrade your browser</a>
to improve your experience and security.</p>
<![endif]-->
```

This is basically to advise users with Internet Explorer 9 or lower to update their internet browser. You don't need to change the code.

```
<!-- Add your site or application content here -->
 <p>Hello world! This is HTML5 Boilerplate.</p>
```

This is our content. We'll edit this part of the HTML to add element and content in our HTML page. You can remove the <p> element since we don't need it.

The following code contains a list of the JavaScript plugins that are linked to our page:

```
<script src="js/vendor/modernizr-3.5.0.min.js"></script>
<script src="https://code.jquery.com/jquery-3.2.1.min.js"
integrity="sha256-hwg4gsxgFZhOsEEamdOYGBf13FyQuiTwlAQgxVSNgt4="
crossorigin="anonymous"></script>
<script>window.jQuery || document.write('<script
src="js/vendor/jquery-3.2.1.min.js"><\/script>')</script>
<script src="js/plugins.js"></script>
<script src="js/main.js"></script>

<!-- Google Analytics: change UA-XXXXX-Y to be your site's ID. -->
<script>
    window.ga=function(){ga.q.push(arguments)};ga.q=[];ga.l=+new Date;
    ga('create','UA-XXXXX-Y','auto');ga('send','pageview')
</script>
<script src="https://www.google-analytics.com/analytics.js" async
defer></script>
```

The plugins are as follows:

- `modernizr`: Detects our user's browser and changes the website's behavior accordingly.
- `Jquery`: We will use this framework to create interaction and animation in our next chapter.
- `Plugin.js`: Contains all the other plugins that we will need.
- `Main.js`: Contains all the JS code we will create.
- `Google Analytics`: An analytics plugin for analyzing users and to help understand how your website is performing. We'll go through this in `Chapter 10`, *Optimizing and Launching Our Website*.

Let's start editing our web page!

Creating our web page

Now that everything is set up, let's get started with putting together our images folder and installing our fonts.

Images folder

I have prepared a folder with all the images that you'll need to do this exercise. Those images can be found in `Resources | Image Web project`. You can simply copy all the images and assets to the `img` folder in our new project folder.

Installing our font

If you have a second look at the website, you can see that we're using custom fonts, which means that we're not using web *safe* fonts. Web-safe fonts are the fonts pre-installed on every device. They appear on all operating systems. This collection of fonts is used by Windows, Mac, Google, Linux, Unix, and so on.

There may be a few more, but this is a list of the common web-safe fonts:

- Arial
- Helvetica
- Times New Roman
- Courier New
- Courier
- Verdana
- Georgia
- Comic Sans MS
- Trebuchet MS
- Arial Black
- Impact

Not super appealing; let's be honest.

But, with CSS3, we can now add our own custom fonts, by using `@font-face`. Let's see how we can add this:

```
@font-face
```

For this exercise, I have provided a zip file called `fonts.zip` to make it easier for you. You can unzip this file and move the folder fonts to our `Web Project` folder. Let's see what's in this folder:

built_titling_el-webfont.woff	Today, 1:16 am	28 KB	Document
built_titling_el-webfont.woff2	Today, 1:16 am	23 KB	Document
built_titling_rg-webfont.woff	Today, 1:16 am	27 KB	Document
built_titling_rg-webfont.woff2	Today, 1:16 am	22 KB	Document
font.css	Today, 5:30 pm	533 bytes	CSS

It contains the font files needed and ready to use for the web.

 To use a custom font on the web, we need to generate or convert this font to a webfont beforehand. You can use the website `fontsquirrel.com` to generate web fonts from your own fonts.

There is also a CSS file that uses the `@font-face` property:

```
@font-face {
  font-family: 'built_titling';
  src: url('built_titling_rg-webfont.woff2') format('woff2'),
       url('built_titling_rg-webfont.woff') format('woff');
  font-weight: 400;
  font-style: normal;
}

@font-face {
  font-family: 'built_titling';
  src: url('built_titling_el-webfont.woff2') format('woff2'),
       url('built_titling_el-webfont.woff') format('woff');
  font-weight: 200;
  font-style: normal;
}
```

So, let's link this CSS file to our HTML file. And in our `index.html`, let's add the following:

```
<link rel="stylesheet" href="fonts/font.css"> <!-- Font face CSS link -->
<link rel="stylesheet" href="css/normalize.css">
<link rel="stylesheet" href="css/main.css">
```

Great, we have now linked our fonts to our HTML page. Let's now add our second font, which is a Google font.

Importing Google Font

Google, since 2010, has provided a platform for users to discover fonts and use them freely. There are over 800 font families available through Google Font's main website, and we'll use one of them in this exercise.

Google made it very easy to import a font. The following are the steps to incorporate a font on our website:

1. Go to the Google Font website (`https://fonts.google.com/`).
2. Search for our font, **Roboto**, and click on the corresponding font (`https://fonts.google.com/specimen/Roboto`).
3. Click on **SELECT THIS FONT.**
4. Click on the little popup at the bottom and switch to the **CUSTOMIZE** tab.
5. We want to have regular and bold.
6. Switch back to the **EMBED** tab and copy the code displayed:

```
<link href="https://fonts.googleapis.com/css?family=Roboto:400,700"
rel="stylesheet">
```

7. Copy and paste this code just before our previous CSS link:

```
<link href="https://fonts.googleapis.com/css?family=Roboto:400,700"
rel="stylesheet">
<link rel="stylesheet" href="fonts/font.css"> <!-- Font face CSS
link -->
```

You have now your Google Font installed!

Now, to use our Google Font, simply paste the CSS property on the element we want to stylize:

```
font-family: 'Roboto', sans-serif;
```

Let's go to our CSS file, located in css | main.css.

Find the section with the following comment:

```
/*
===========================================================================
    Author's custom styles
===========================================================================
*/
```

Here, write:

```
body {
  font-family: 'Roboto', sans-serif;
}
```

This will apply the font-family property to the `<body>` element, which is the main element of our HTML page, so it will be applied to all elements inside `<body>`.

Adding normalize.css

You probably noticed another `css` file when looking for the `main.css`. What is `normalize.css` and why should we integrate this with our HTML?

As we saw earlier, every browser does not render the same. With `normalize.css`, all browsers will render elements more consistently and in line with modern standards. We simply need to add it to our other `css` files and it will do the job. Cool, isn't it?

The header

Let's start implementing our header. Best practice is to first do the HTML and then finish with the CSS. Let's have a look at our design first.

As you can see, our header has a transparent background, with a logo and main menu on the left-hand side, and a secondary menu on the right-hand side.

First, create a `<header>` tag in our HTML document:

```
<!-- Add your site or application content here --> <header></header>
```

Creating a menu

To create our menu, we need to create a list. In HTML, to create a list you have to use the tag `<ul>`.

`<ul>` stands for unordered list; it needs to have a list tag inside `<li>`. You can use it as follows:

```
<ul>
  <li>Coffee</li>
  <li>Tea</li>
  <li>Milk</li>
</ul>
```

Our list should end up looking like this:

```
<header>
  <ul>
    <li>Upcoming events</li>
    <li>Past events</li>
    <li>FAQ</li>
    <li>About us</li>
    <li>Blog</li>
    <li>Contact</li>
  </ul>
</header>
```

Inserting links

To make the menu work, we need to add links to our list; otherwise, it will go nowhere. To add a link, you have to use the tag `<a>`. To make each `<li>` element clickable as a link, we need to add the `<a>` tag inside the `<li>` tag, as follows:

```
<li><a>Upcoming events</a></li>
```

Now we need to specify where the link goes. For that, we need to add the attribute `href`:

```
<li><a href="upcoming.html">Upcoming events</a></li>
```

If the `href` attribute is not present, the `<a>` tag won't act as a hyperlink. The value of `href` can be an absolute link to another website or a relative link to a file on the same domain. It's basically the same behavior as the `src` attribute we saw earlier.

In the end, our menu should look like this:

```
<ul>
  <li><a href="upcoming.html">Upcoming events</a></li>
  <li><a href="past.html">Past events</a></li>
  <li><a href="faq.html">FAQ</a></li>
  <li><a href="about.html">About us</a></li>
```

```
    <li><a href="blog.html">Blog</a></li>
    <li><a href="contact.html">Contact</a></li>
</ul>
```

Lastly, let's add a class to our `<ul>` tag so we can specify the style later on with `css`, like this:

```
<ul class="main-nav">
```

Adding a logo

In addition to our navigation, we also have a logo on the left-hand side. I have provided some assets you can use for this exercise in the `Resources` folder (`Exercise 2 | Assets`).

Simply copy and paste the `logo.png` and `logo@2x.png` files into your `img` folder on your `Web Project`.

`logo@2x.png` is simply the retina version of the image, which means it has double the pixel density of the normal image. It's a good practice to name your retina image with the suffix `@2x`.

Now we'll simply add an image before our menu, as follows:

```
<img src="img/logo.png" alt="">
```

Perhaps you have noticed that we only put `logo.png` and there is no use of the `logo@2x.png`. To be able to use our retina version image only on retina devices, we'll have to use the attribute `srcset`:

```
<img src="img/logo.png" srcset="img/logo.png 1x, img/logo@2x.png 2x">
```

`srcset` attribute is pretty simple to use. For each asset, add the density at the end to specify which screen density it should be used. In this example, we'll put `img/logo@2x.png 2x`. You can also specify at which screen width it should appear, but let's keep it simple for this example.

One web design good practice is to make the logo link to the homepage. To do so, we need to put the img tag inside a tag:

```
<a href="#"><img src="img/logo.png" srcset="img/logo.png 1x,
img/logo@2x.png 2x"></a>
```

To make sure the link is landing on the website's homepage, we need to change the href attribute "#" to "/" so it will go to the root of the folder:

```
<a href="/"><img src="img/logo.png" srcset="img/logo.png 1x,
img/logo@2x.png 2x"></a>
```

Lastly, let's put a class "logo" so we can target this element later:

```
<a class="logo" href="/"><img src="img/logo.png" srcset="img/logo.png 1x,
img/logo@2x.png 2x"></a>
```

Right-hand side menu

The last part of the menu is the right-hand side menu with the Login and Facebook like buttons. There are many ways to do it, but I suggest using another list such as the previous one we created:

```
<ul class="right-nav">
  <li><a href="login.html">Login</a></li>
  <li><a href="#">Facebook</a></li>
</ul>
```

We'll add the class "right-nav" and add 2 <li>, as shown in the preceding code.

Adding a Facebook like button

To add the Facebook like button, we first need to create the button. To do so, we need to go to the Facebook Developer's website to get the information. I have the link handy for you: https://developers.facebook.com/docs/plugins/like-button. On this page, you'll find the means to customize your button, as shown in the following screenshot:

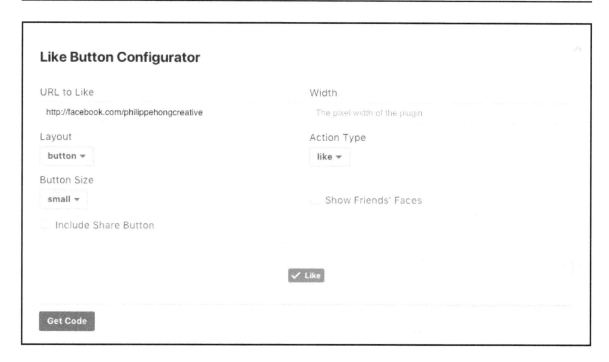

Once done, click on **Get Code** and select the tab **IFrame:**

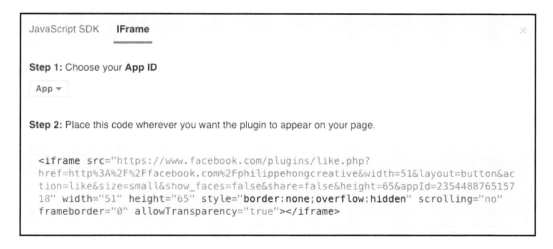

We can copy this piece of code into our website in our second `<li>` tag.

We're going to customize the button a bit; change the default value of the attribute height to 20px. You should end up with code like this:

```
<ul class="right-nav">
  <li><a href="login.html">Login</a></li>
  <li><a href="#"><iframe
src="https://www.facebook.com/plugins/like.php?href=http%3A%2F%2Ffacebook.c
om%2Fphilippehongcreative&width=51&layout=button&action=like&size=small&sho
w_faces=false&share=false&height=65&appId=235448876515718" width="51"
height="20" style="border:none;overflow:hidden" scrolling="no"
frameborder="0" allowTransparency="true"></iframe></a></li>
</ul>
```

We have now our menu in HTML; let's add some styling with CSS to make it look better.

Styling our header

At the moment, our header is looking very boring. But, no worries, we'll add some magic with CSS and make it prettier.

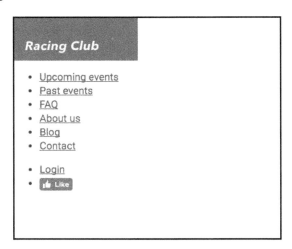

We saw earlier that CSS can be written in three different ways:

- Inside an HTML Tag with a `style` attribute
- Inside our `<head>` section in a HTML document with the tag `<style>`
- CSS code can also be put into an external file

For our own project, we're going to use the third way, as commonly used in the web in general, because the CSS can be changed without changing the HTML file.

Let's create our CSS file that will be used for our general styling. In Atom, click **File** | **New File**, and save the file with **File** | **Save As**. Choose the folder `css` and name this file `styles.css`. We have to link this file as we did with the `font.css` file we created earlier:

```
<link href="https://fonts.googleapis.com/css?family=Roboto:400,700"
rel="stylesheet">
<link rel="stylesheet" href="fonts/fonts.css"> <!-- Font face CSS link -->
<link rel="stylesheet" href="css/normalize.css">
<link rel="stylesheet" href="css/main.css">
<link rel="stylesheet" href="css/styles.css">
```

Now that we have our `styles.css`, we can get started. But I usually like to view both HTML and CSS at the same time. It's easy to do so; select your `styles.css`, then go to **View** | **Panes** | **Split Right**. You now have the file open on two different panes. You can close the one on the left:

The view split in two in Atom.

First, we need to target the header tag. The header tag has no class, but we can target an HTML tag with just this tag. In CSS it will be:

```
header {
}
```

This will basically target every <header> tag in the HTML, so you need to be careful about it:

If we take a look closely at our design, we can notice that the header takes the full width of the web page, has a height of *70px*, and has a gradient grey to a transparent background that lets the image appear behind it.

To do so we have the CSS property width:

```
header {
    width: 100%;
    height: 70px;
}
```

We can now add the background gradient. For that, we have the CSS property background-image: linear-gradient:

```
background-image: linear-gradient(0deg, rgba(0,0,0,0.00) 0%,
rgba(0,0,0,0.50) 50%);
```

To create a gradient with CSS, I often use a generator (http://www.colorzilla.com/gradient-editor/) that creates the final code for me.

I also sometimes use the CSS tool provided by Sketch or Photoshop to copy the CSS property straight from the design.

For this exercise, you can just copy the code I provided:

```
header {
    width: 100%;
    background-image: linear-gradient(0deg, rgba(0,0,0,0.00) 0%,
rgba(0,0,0,0.50) 50%);
}
```

Save both CSS and HTML files and open `index.html` on your browser:

We now have our container, but we still need to stylize our menu. Let's first target our list by its class, `main-nav`. If you remember, to call a class, we need to add a dot before the name of the class, like this:

```
header .main-nav {

}
```

Now we want to specifically target every `<li>` inside the `<ul>`. To do so, we simply have to add `li` after, as we saw in the chapter earlier:

```
header .main-nav li {

}
```

Let's first remove the list styling, which is a circle by default. To do that, we need to use the CSS property `list-style-type`:

```
header .main-nav li {
  list-style-type: none;
}
```

Let's put `none`, so it will remove all styling in the `li` tag.

We also have to display the list horizontally instead of vertically. To make this happen, we need to use the CSS property `display: inline-block`.

The CSS property `display: inline-block` will display the list as inline but with the ability to set width and height as a block element:

```
header .main-nav li {
  list-style-type: none;
  display: inline-block;
}
```

Let's save our work and check to see what we have so far:

Our goal now is to put the menu right next to the logo. For that, we'll need to make the logo float. As we saw earlier in the CSS chapter, we'll use the CSS property `float: left;` on the logo:

```
header .logo {
    float: left;
}
```

We now need to display the menu correctly. We'll first add a height to our `main-nav`:

```
header .main-nav {
    height: 70px;
}
```

We also need to make the menu float so the right-hand menu can come on top:

```
header .main-nav {
    height: 70px;
}
```

Since all `<ul>` tags have some padding and margin by default, we need to overwrite that:

```
Header .main-nav {
    height: 70px;
    float: left;
    margin: 0;
    padding: 0;
}
```

The problem is that we have the menu side by side with the logo, so we need to add some padding to the menu:

```
header .main-nav {
  height: 70px;
  float: left;
  margin: 0;
  padding: 0;
  padding-left: 0;
}
```

But now we have two properties that are overlapping since padding includes all paddings such as padding-left. This will still work but it's bad CSS. To write it properly, we can combine and modify the paddings with just one CSS property:

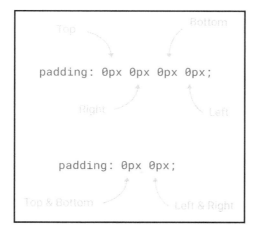

This image explains how you can change different paddings with just one property.

For our exercise, we will do the following:

```
header .main-nav {
  height: 70px;
  float: left;
  margin: 0;
  padding: 0px 15px;
}
```

Our next goal is to make our menu vertically aligned with the logo. To do so, we can use a little CSS hack by using line-height, which is used normally to change the space between lines on a paragraph. By setting the `line-height` to the height of the menu, we'll make the menu vertically aligned:

```
header .main-nav {
   height: 70px;
   float: left;
   margin: 0;
   padding: 0px 15px;
   line-height: 70px;
}
```

Now let's customize the font to the one we installed earlier. Let me show you the final CSS so that I can explain line by line what, exactly, it means:

```
header .main-nav li a {
   color: white;
   text-decoration: none;
   font-family: 'built_titling', Helvetica, sans-serif;
   font-weight: 200;
   font-size: 20px;
   letter-spacing: 4px;
   padding: 0px 15px;
}
```

First we need to target the `<a>` tag in our `.main-nav` class. Inside our bracket, we'll have the following:

1. `color: white;` will specify the color of the text. You can set this color with a HEX code or with the 140 native color CSS support (`https://www.w3schools.com/cssref/css_colors.asp`).
2. `text-decoration: none;` will suppress all decoration on the text. Here we want to suppress the underline on every link.
3. `font-family: 'built_titling', Helvetica, sans-serif;` is to specify the font we want to display. The following font name will serve if the first one couldn't load.
4. `font-weight: 200;` is the level of bold of the font.
5. `font-size: 20px;` will be the size of the font in pixels.
6. `letter-spacing:` will indicate the spacing between each character.
7. `padding:` it's inside-padding as we learned earlier.

We're almost done. Let's save and have a look:

We have only the right-hand part to finish, let's get this done!

For this part, we'll need to make it float on the right. Let's first target this class:

```
Header .right-nav {

}
```

This right nav will follow almost the same properties as the left nav; we'll only change the float to right:

```
header .right-nav {
    height: 70px;
    float: right;
    margin: 0;
    padding: 0px 15px;
    line-height: 70px;
}
```

As you will see, we'll use a lot of copy/paste for coding as a lot of elements will use the same properties.

But what if we have a lot of selectors that use the same CSS properties? Do we have to copy/paste all of them? A good practice in coding is always to simplify our code so that it takes less time to load.

In CSS, we can call on multiple selectors and put the same CC properties. To do so, we need to separate them with a comma `,`. For our `left-nav` and `right-nav` for example, we can do the following:

```
header .main-nav, header .right-nav{
    height: 70px;
    float: left;
    margin: 0;
    padding: 0px 15px;
    line-height: 70px;
}
```

```
header .right-nav {
  float: right;
}
```

This will have the same effect as the code we wrote before. And because we call `.right-nav` and put the property `float: right;` after, it overwrites the previous property, which was `float: left;`. This is a good practice to have when coding in CSS.

Let's make the rest of the code with this good practice in mind:

```
header .main-nav li, header .right-nav li {
  list-style-type: none;
  display: inline-block;
}

header .main-nav li a, header .right-nav li a {
  color: white;
  text-decoration: none;
  font-family: 'built_titling', Helvetica, sans-serif;
  font-weight: 200;
  font-size: 20px;
  letter-spacing: 4px;
  padding: 0px 15px;
}
```

We now have our header. Let's save it and have a final look:

Fantastic! Lastly, to make our code clean and easy to read, I'll advise putting some comments at the beginning and at the end of each section of your code.

This will be the final CSS code for our HEADER section:

```
/* HEADER */

header {
  width: 100%;
  height: 70px;
  background-image: linear-gradient(0deg, rgba(0,0,0,0.00) 0%,
rgba(0,0,0,0.50) 50%);
  position: absolute;
}
```

```
header .logo {
  float: left;
}

header .main-nav, header .right-nav{
  height: 70px;
  float: left;
  margin: 0;
  padding: 0px 15px;
  line-height: 70px;
}

header .right-nav {
  float: right;
}

header .main-nav li, header .right-nav li {
  list-style-type: none;
  display: inline-block;
}

header .main-nav li a, header .right-nav li a {
  color: white;
  text-decoration: none;
  font-family: 'built_titling', Helvetica, sans-serif;
  font-weight: 200;
  font-size: 20px;
  letter-spacing: 4px;
  padding: 0px 15px;
}

/* END OF HEADER */
```

Adding the hero section

After implementing our header, we can now go the next step, which is the hero Section. The hero section is, in web design, usually composed with a big image, a title, a description, and a **Call to Action** (CTA). It serves as an overview of the website because it's the first thing the visitor will see.

In our design, we have the following:

It's quite simple. It's composed of a background image, with a gradient overlay and some text with a button on the left. If we try to mark out the outline of each block, we could have something like this:

Maybe this can help you visualize what we're trying to do in HTML/CSS. Let's start with the HTML:

We can start first by creating a section (purple) that will hold everything:

```
<section id="hero">
</section>
```

We'll add an `id` so it's easier to call upon it later.

We now have to create a `container` (fuschia) that will contain all the elements inside but also be centered horizontally. For that, we'll create a `div` with the class `container`:

```
<section id="hero">
  <div class="container">
  </div>
</section>
```

Inside we'll have a block that will contain the title, description, and button, which will be left aligned. We can call it `"hero-text"`:

```
<section id="hero">
  <div class="container">
    <div class="hero-text">
    </div>
  </div>
</section>
```

Now, let's add the content inside:

```
<section id="hero">
  <div class="container">
    <div class="hero-text">
      <p class="hero-date">10.05.18</p>
      <h1 class="hero-title">Wakefield Park</h1>
      <button type="button" name="button" class="btn-primary">Book
now</button>
    </div>
  </div>
</section>
```

As you might have seen, we didn't add the image in the HTML, because we want to add it with CSS. Adding images with CSS allows more flexibility and customization. In this case, we want to make it full screen and to cover the background. First, let's call our #hero div:

```
#hero {

}
```

Let's add the following styling:

```
#hero {
  width: 100%;
  height: 700px;
  background-image:
    linear-gradient(to bottom, rgba(0,0,0,0.3) 0%,rgba(0,0,0,0.4) 100%),
    url("../img/hero-image.jpg");
  background-repeat: no-repeat;
  background-size: cover;
  background-position: center;
}
```

Here are some explanations:

1. We first need to set the size of the block. As we want it to be full screen, we have to make the width 100 percent and the height 700px, as the dimension is the design.
2. With CSS5, we have the ability to add multiple backgrounds. For that, we need to separate them with a comma, as shown previously.
3. We use `background-repeat` to make the background not repeat indefinitely as per default.

4. `background-size: cover;` will make the background image stretch following the size of the block, here the full screen.

5. `background-position: center;` will always put the background in the center, even when resizing.

6. Let's save our files and see what we get:

We have our image and gradient; let's now move into our content.

As we said earlier, we need our content to be centered. As you may have spotted, our design follows a grid:

We need to create this container, which has a width of 940px and is centered horizontally. For that it's very simple, all we'll need to do is:

```css
.container {
  max-width: 940px;
  margin: 0 auto;
}
```

Here are some notes:

1. `max-width: 940px::` we don't want the container to be more than `940px`, but it can be less than that depending on screen size.
2. `margin: 0 auto;` is a simple way to horizontally center a block element.

The next step will be to stylise the content. But, first, we need to analyze the design before jumping into the code. When looking at the design, we can see that:

- The hero content needs to be vertically centered from the hero section
- The hero content needs to be aligned on the left and have a width of 50 percent

CSS flexbox

To make that happen, we'll use the new CSS property `display: flex`. CSS flexbox is very practical because it allows you to position element very easily. Centering, ordering, and aligning is made very easy with flexbox. If you can handle this new property, I guarantee you'll be a killer in CSS.

In our case, we want our `.container` to be centered vertically. To do that, we'll target the class and add these properties:

```
#hero .container {
  display: flex;
  align-items: center;
  height: 700px;
}
```

By adding `#hero` before `.container`, we're targeting only elements with the class `.container` inside `#hero`. We don't want all `.container` to have the same properties:

1. `display: flex;` has to be set on the parent element.
2. `align-items: center;` will vertically align and center all elements inside this element. Magic!
3. The `height` needs to be set so you can align the elements in the middle.

 CSS flexbox has very powerful properties. We could have done the entire website with flexbox properties, but for you to learn all the possibilities, we had to go through all the steps.

Let's continue with our text styling:

```
.hero-text {
  max-width: 470px;
}
```

We set this width because we don't want the text to go all the way to the right, so we set the max-width to half of the `.container`'s `max-width`. Continue to follow our design:

```css
.hero-text .hero-date {
  font-family: 'built_titling', Helvetica, sans-serif;
  font-size: 30px;
  color: #FFFFFF;
  font-weight: normal;
}
```

Next, we have our title:

```css
.hero-text .hero-title {
  font-family: 'built_titling', Helvetica, sans-serif;
  font-size: 120px;
  margin: 20px 0px;
  font-weight: normal;
  color: #FFFFFF;
  line-height: 1;
}
```

Lastly, we have our button:

```css
.btn-primary {
  display: inline-block;
  font-family: 'built_titling', Helvetica, sans-serif;
  font-weight: 400;
  font-size: 18px;
  letter-spacing: 4.5px;
  background: #BF0000;
  color: white;
  padding: 12px 22px;
  border: none;
  outline: none;
}
```

We use `display: inline-block;` so we can use the button as an inline element but with the characteristic of a block element (width and height). `border` and `outline` are set to `none` by default. Every button has a `border` and `outline`.

Let's see what we have:

The website is looking great, but we have some annoying margins at the top. To fix this, we need to use the CSS property "`position`".

Positioning in CSS

In CSS, there are five different position values:

- Static
- Relative
- Fixed
- Absolute
- Sticky

Position static

They all have different usages. All HTML elements are positioned static by default.

Position relative

An element with the position relative is positioned relatively to its normal position. You adjust the positioning by changing its left, top, right, or bottom position.

For example:

```
div.relative-element {
    position: relative;
    top: 50px;
    left: 50px;
}
```

Check the following diagram for better understanding:

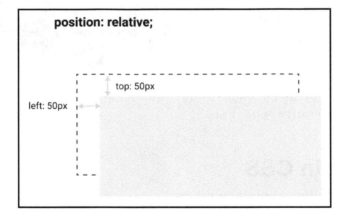

Position absolute

An element with the position absolute will be positioned next to its nearest positioned parent, which means any element with a position that expects position static. If this element has no parent, it will be positioned to the viewport itself.

A positioned absolute element will be placed over the parent element.

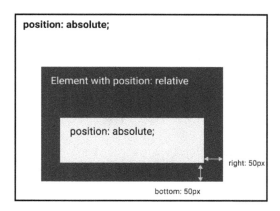

Position fixed

An element with the position fixed will act as a position absolute but only with the viewport itself. It will stay in the same position even if the page is scrolled:

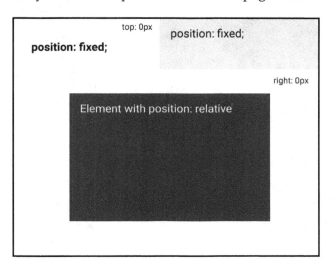

Position sticky

An element with the position sticky is positioned based on the user's scroll position.

It's not fully supported in every browser, however, so we will not use it in this exercise.

Now that we understand the usage of a position in CSS, we need to make the header superimposed on to the hero section. To do that, we need to make the header position absolute. As the header has no parent element, it will be positioned on the viewport itself.

Let's go back to the header section and add the position: absolute property:

```
header {
  width: 100%;
  height: 70px;
  background-image: linear-gradient(0deg, rgba(0,0,0,0.00) 0%,
rgba(0,0,0,0.50) 50%);
  position: absolute;
}
```

Let's save and see what we have:

We have now our first section and header well implemented. Let's continue to the next section.

Blog section

First, as we always do (and you need to get into this habit), we need to analyze the design and see how is it composed:

As we can see, the **Blog** section is composed of a header and six **Blog** posts. There are two rows of three posts each, with an equal width of one-third.

We know how to design this with a `float` and the `display: inline-block` properties. Let's try to build it with CSS flexbox.

Let's first add the HTML:

```
<section id="blog">
  <div class="container">
    <h2><b>Blog</b> Everything about RACING CLUB</h2>

  </div>
</section>
```

Here are some explanations:

1. We need to create another `section id "blog"`
2. We need to reuse the class `container` to have a container that follows the same width
3. We add an `<h2>` since it's not as important as the hero title
4. We add a `<b>` tag to make the word **Blog** bold

Let's add our `blog` posts section now:

```
<section id="blog">
  <div class="container">
    <h2><b>Blog</b> Everything about RACING CLUB</h2>
    <div class="blog-posts">
      <div class="blog-post">
        <img src="img/blog-img/blog1.jpg" srcset="img/blog-img/blog1.jpg
1x, img/blog-img/blog1@2x.jpg 2x">
        <p class="blog-post-date">09th January 2016</p>
        <h3>Racing Club Advan Neova Challenge Round 3 Update</h3>
        <p class="blog-post-desc">FINAL ROUND: Labour Day Trackday
Wakefield Park. Last chance to compete in the Circuit Club Advan Neova
Challenge 2016!
There was much anticipation with Jason's big power Evo competing at Round
3, however some suspected engi... <a href="#">Read More</a></p>
      </div>
    </div>
  </div>
</section>
```

Here is what we did:

1. We added a `div` with the class `"blog-posts"` that contains all the **Blog** posts.

2. Inside, we create a div with the class "`blog-post`", which will be a single blog post.

3. Inside this `div`, we added the image with the `img` tag and `srcset` we learned earlier.

4. We also added a p tag with a class "`blog-post-date`" for the **Blog** post date.

5. We added a `<h3>` without class because it's the only `h3` element, so we can target it easily with CSS.

6. Lastly, we added the `description` text with a link inside.

This represents a single **Blog** post, so to make six of them, we simply need to duplicate the `blog` post element six times.

Let's also add another `div` to make our **Show More** button:

```
<div class="blog-show-more">
  <button type="button" name="button" class="btn-primary">More
posts</button>
</div>
```

In the end, you should have something like this:

```
<section id="blog">
  <div class="container">
    <h2><b>Blog</b> Everything about RACING CLUB</h2>
    <div class="blog-posts">

      <div class="blog-post">
        <img src="img/blog-img/blog1.jpg" srcset="img/blog-img/blog1.jpg
1x, img/blog-img/blog1@2x.jpg 2x">
        <p class="blog-post-date">09th January 2016</p>
        <h3>Racing Club Advan Neova Challenge Round 3 Update</h3>
        <p class="blog-post-desc">FINAL ROUND: Labour Day Trackday
Wakefield Park. Last chance to compete in the Circuit Club Advan Neova
Challenge 2016!
There was much anticipation with Jason's big power Evo competing at Round
3, however some suspected engi... <a href="#">Read More</a></p>
      </div>

      <div class="blog-post">
        <img src="img/blog-img/blog2.jpg" srcset="img/blog-img/blog2.jpg
1x, img/blog-img/blog2@2x.jpg 2x">
        <p class="blog-post-date">09th January 2016</p>
        <h3>Hidden Behind the Scenes</h3>
        <p class="blog-post-desc">Originally posted by Narada Kudinar,
23.08.11.
```

```
At our Trackdays, we get a variety - owners with their girlfriends, owners
with their mates, owners and their mechanics - but there is one combination
I am truly at envy with. It's the owners and their Dads. <a href="#">Read
More</a></p>
        </div>

    <div class="blog-post">
        <img src="img/blog-img/blog3.jpg" srcset="img/blog-img/blog3.jpg
1x, img/blog-img/blog3@2x.jpg 2x">
        <p class="blog-post-date">04th July 2015</p>
        <h3>Introducing Advan Trackdays!</h3>
        <p class="blog-post-desc">For the first time, Yokohama Advan Tyres
are hosting their very own Trackdays, hosted by your's truly! The aim? To
thank their loyal customers by providing a bargain event as well as
introduce new Advan tyres to those who don't use them yet...<a
href="#">Read More</a></p>
        </div>

    <div class="blog-post">
        <img src="img/blog-img/blog4.jpg" srcset="img/blog-img/blog4.jpg
1x, img/blog-img/blog4@2x.jpg 2x">
        <p class="blog-post-date">09th Jun 2015</p>
        <h3>ANZAC Day Spots Running Out!</h3>
        <p class="blog-post-desc">FINAL ROUND: Labour Day Trackday
Wakefield Park. Last chance to compete in the Circuit Club Advan Neova
Challenge 2016!
There was much anticipation with Jason's big power Evo competing at Round
3, however some suspected engi... <a href="#">Read More</a></p>
        </div>

    <div class="blog-post">
        <img src="img/blog-img/blog5.jpg" srcset="img/blog-img/blog5.jpg
1x, img/blog-img/blog5@2x.jpg 2x">
        <p class="blog-post-date">15th Mar 2015</p>
        <h3>10 Year Anniversary Details Now Available!</h3>
        <p class="blog-post-desc">Originally posted by Narada Kudinar,
23.08.11.
At our Trackdays, we get a variety - owners with their girlfriends, owners
with their mates, owners and their mechanics - but there is one combination
I am truly at envy with. It's the owners and their Dads. <a href="#">Read
More</a></p>
        </div>

    <div class="blog-post">
        <img src="img/blog-img/blog6.jpg" srcset="img/blog-img/blog6.jpg
1x, img/blog-img/blog6@2x.jpg 2x">
        <p class="blog-post-date">16th Jan 2015</p>
        <h3>Prepare for EPICNESS</h3>
```

```
    <p class="blog-post-desc">For the first time, Yokohama Advan Tyres
are hosting their very own Trackdays, hosted by your's truly! The aim? To
thank their loyal customers by providing a bargain event as well as
introduce new Advan tyres to those who don't use them yet... <a
href="#">Read More</a></p>
    </div>

  </div>
div class="blog-show-more">
    <button type="button" name="button" class="btn-primary">More
posts</button>
  </div>

 </div>
</section>
```

Let's head to the CSS now! We will style the title first:

```
#blog h2 {
  font-family: 'built_titling', Helvetica, sans-serif;
  font-weight: 200;
  font-size: 60px;
}
```

For the `blog-posts` container, we'll do as follows:

```
.blog-posts {
  display: flex;
  flex-direction: row;
  flex-wrap: wrap;
  margin-top: 50px;
}

.blog-post {
  width: 33.33%;
  padding: 0 5px;
  box-sizing: border-box;
  margin-bottom: 30px;
}
```

`.blog-posts` is the parent element and `.blog-post` is the child element.

Here is some information regarding `.blog-posts`:

1. `display: flex;` always needs to be added to the parent element.
2. `flex-direction: row;` will direct the child elements as a row. You can put it as a column if you want.

3. `flex-wrap: wrap;` will make the child elements wrap onto multiple lines, from top to bottom. By default, it will try to fit every element on to one line.
4. `margin-top: 50px;` adds a bit of margin on the top.

Here is some information regarding `.blog-post`:

1. `width: 33.33%;` sets the width as one-third of the total width
2. `padding: 0 5px;` adds some padding on the right and left sides
3. `box-sizing: border-box;:` as we saw earlier, this makes the padding and margin properties apply inside the box instead of outside

So far, we have the right layout:

BLOG EVERYTHING ABOUT RACING CLUB

09th January 2016

Racing Club Advan Neova Challenge Round 3 Update

FINAL ROUND: Labour Day Trackday Wakefield Park. Last chance to compete in the Circuit Club Advan Neova Challenge 2016! There was much anticipation with Jason's big power Evo competing at Round 3, however some suspected engi... Read More

09th January 2016

Hidden Behind the Scenes

Originally posted by Narada Kudinar, 23.08.11. At our Trackdays, we get a variety - owners with their girlfriends, owners with their mates, owners and their mechanics - but there is one combination I am truly at envy with. It's the owners and their Dads. Read More

04th July 2015

Introducing Advan Trackdays!

For the first time, Yokohama Advan Tyres are hosting their very own Trackdays, hosted by your's truly! The aim? To thank their loyal customers by providing a bargain event as well as introduce new Advan tyres to those who don't use them yet...Read More

09th Jun 2015

ANZAC Day Spots Running Out!

FINAL ROUND: Labour Day Trackday Wakefield Park. Last chance to compete in the Circuit Club Advan Neova Challenge 2016! There was much anticipation with Jason's big power Evo competing at Round 3, however some suspected engi... Read More

15th Mar 2015

10 Year Anniversary Details Now Available!

Originally posted by Narada Kudinar, 23.08.11. At our Trackdays, we get a variety - owners with their girlfriends, owners with their mates, owners and their mechanics - but there is one combination I am truly at envy with. It's the owners and their Dads. Read More

16th Jan 2015

Prepare for EPICNESS

For the first time, Yokohama Advan Tyres are hosting their very own Trackdays, hosted by your's truly! The aim? To thank their loyal customers by providing a bargain event as well as introduce new Advan tyres to those who don't use them yet... Read More

Let's style the content inside a **Blog** post:

```
.blog-post img {
  width: 100%;
}
```

We use `width: 100%;` as we want our images to take `100%` of the `width`. The rest is pretty basic CSS, just to follow the design:

```
.blog-post .blog-post-date {
  font-size: 14px;
  color: #9A9A9A;
  margin-top: 20px;
}

.blog-post h3 {
  font-size: 20px;
  color: #4A4A4A;
  letter-spacing: -0.4px;
  line-height: 1.4;
}


.blog-post .blog-post-desc {
  font-size: 14px;
  color: #4A4A4A;
  line-height: 1.6;
}

.blog-post .blog-post-desc a {
  color: #BF0000;
  text-decoration: underline;
  font-weight: bold;
}
```

Here's what we end up with:

BLOG EVERYTHING ABOUT RACING CLUB

09th January 2016

Racing Club Advan Neova Challenge Round 3 Update

FINAL ROUND: Labour Day Trackday Wakefield Park. Last chance to compete in the Circuit Club Advan Neova Challenge 2016! There was much anticipation with Jason's big power Evo competing at Round 3, however some suspected engi... **Read More**

09th January 2016

Hidden Behind the Scenes

Originally posted by Narada Kudinar, 23.08.11. At our Trackdays, we get a variety - owners with their girlfriends, owners with their mates, owners and their mechanics - but there is one combination I am truly in envy with. It's the owners and their Dads. **Read More**

04th July 2015

Introducing Advan Trackdays!

For the first time, Yokohama Advan Tyres are hosting their very own Trackdays, hosted by your's truly! The aim? To thank their loyal customers by providing a bargain event as well as introduce new Advan tyres to those who don't use them yet...**Read More**

09th Jun 2015

ANZAC Day Spots Running Out!

FINAL ROUND: Labour Day Trackday Wakefield Park. Last chance to compete in the Circuit Club Advan Neova Challenge 2016! There was much anticipation with Jason's big power Evo competing at Round 3, however some suspected engi... **Read More**

15th Mar 2015

10 Year Anniversary Details Now Available!

Originally posted by Narada Kudinar, 23.08.11. At our Trackdays, we get a variety - owners with their girlfriends, owners with their mates, owners and their mechanics - but there is one combination I am truly in envy with. It's the owners and their Dads. **Read More**

16th Jan 2015

Prepare for EPICNESS

For the first time, Yokohama Advan Tyres are hosting their very own Trackdays, hosted by your's truly! The aim? To thank their loyal customers by providing a bargain event as well as introduce new Advan tyres to those who don't use them yet... **Read More**

It's looking quite similar to me now. The last part is the **Show More** button. A simple hack would be to add a `text-align: center` to the parent element so it will make the button aligned in the middle:

```
.blog-show-more {
  text-align: center;
}
```

For the last touch, I'll add some margins at the bottom to add a bit of white space:

```
#blog {
  margin-bottom: 50px;
}
```

Our CSS for the `blog` section:

```
/* BLOG SECTION */

#blog {
  margin-bottom: 50px;
}

#blog h2 {
  font-family: 'built_titling', Helvetica, sans-serif;
  font-weight: 200;
  font-size: 60px;
}

.blog-posts {
  display: flex;
  flex-direction: row;
  flex-wrap: wrap;
  margin-top: 50px;
}

.blog-post {
  width: 33.33%;
  padding: 0 5px;
  box-sizing: border-box;
  margin-bottom: 30px;
}

.blog-post img {
  width: 100%;
}

.blog-post .blog-post-date {
  font-size: 14px;
  color: #9A9A9A;
  margin-top: 20px;
}

.blog-post h3 {
  font-size: 20px;
  color: #4A4A4A;
  letter-spacing: -0.4px;
```

```
    line-height: 1.4;
}

.blog-post .blog-post-desc {
  font-size: 14px;
  color: #4A4A4A;
  line-height: 1.6;
}

.blog-post .blog-post-desc a {
  color: #BF0000;
  text-decoration: underline;
  font-weight: bold;
}

.blog-show-more {
  text-align: center;
}


/* END OF BLOG SECTION */
```

Creating the ABOUT US section

This section is not very complex. Let's check out the design:

If we use our block analyzer, we can have something such as this:

What we need to do:

- Make the content vertically centered
- Align the text on the left
- Have a background image covering the entire section

The best way to align elements vertically is, as we saw earlier, to use CSS flexbox.

Let's create our HTML. After our `blog` section, we're going to add our `about-us` section:

```
<section id="about-us">
</section>
```

Inside this section, as usual, we're going to add our `container`:

```
<section id="about-us">
        <div class="container">
        </div>
</section>
```

And inside our container, we'll create our two blocks that will contain our big title and our description:

```
<section id="about-us">
  <div class="container">
    <div class="about-us-title">
        <h3>The love of cars</h3>
```

```
      </div>
      <div class="about-us-desc">
        <h4>About us</h4>
        <p>Racing Club was founded in 2003 with one goal in mind, to make
motorsport accessible through Trackdays. What started out simply as a bunch
of mates with a love of cars and driving fast... </p>
        <button type="button" name="button" class="btn-primary">Learn
more</button>
      </div>
    </div>
  </section>
```

Let's save and jump into our CSS file:

1. First, target our about section ID:

   ```
   #about-us {
   }
   ```

2. Add the background image for our section:

   ```
   #about-us {
     width: 100%;
     background-image: url(../img/about-us-bg.jpg);
     background-repeat: no-repeat;
     background-size: cover;
     padding: 120px 0;
     color: white;
   }
   ```

   We use the same CSS properties that we used previously in our hero section.
   Some padding is added, to remain similar to the design. We set the color at
   the parent level so we don't have to set the color in each child element.

3. Set flexbox in the `container`:

   ```
   #about-us .container {
     display: flex;
     align-items: top;
   }
   ```

   `align-items: top;` will align the text from the `top`, as in the design.

4. We now have to set the `width` of the block inside the container; otherwise, the flexbox will not work:

```
.about-us-title {
  width: 50%;
}

.about-us-desc {
  width: 50%;
}
```

Let's save and check the design:

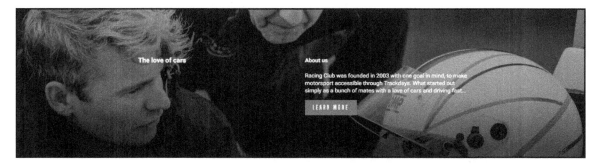

So far, so good; we're heading the right way. Let's add some styles for our title and description.

5. Add styling to our heading:

```
.about-us-title h3 {
  font-family: 'built_titling', Helvetica, sans-serif;
  font-weight: 400;
  font-size: 120px;
  line-height: 1;
  letter-spacing: -1px;
  margin: 0;
}
```

`margin: 0` had to be added by default, as every `h` title has a margin following the size of the text. Let's check again:

We're pretty close, but we still need to be more precise in our implementation:

We can see in our design that we have a few line breaks and a red line at the bottom of the title.

To do that, we'll need to add some break lines with HTML. To add a break line with HTML, we can use the tag `<br />` in any text block. So in our title, we'll add a `<br />` tag after `The` and `love`:

```
<h3>The<br /> love<br /> of cars</h3>
```

Now, to add the red line, we can create a `<div>` and customize it to be the shape and colors we want. But it will add something useless in the HTML.

A better way to do it is to use the `::before`/`::after` selector in CSS. This selector can add some text before or after an HTML element.

It's primarily used to add extra text after a paragraph, but we'll use it to add this red line.

To do so, we have to select the h3 element and add `::after`:

```
.about-us-title h3::after {
}
```

For every `::after` or `::before` selection, we need to add the CSS property `content`:

```
.about-us-title h3::after {
  content: "";
}
```

We'll leave the value blank as we don't want any text. Continue:

```
.about-us-title h3::after {
  content: "";
  display: block;
  background: #BF0000;
  width: 90px;
  height: 2px;
  margin-top: 30px;
}
```

What we did:

- We set the `display` as `block` as it's inline by default
- We added the red background and the dimension
- We added a margin to have some space between the text and the red line

We're almost set. We have a final touch to add to the title of our description:

```css
.about-us-desc h4 {
  font-family: 'built_titling', Helvetica, sans-serif;
  font-weight: 400;
  font-size: 26px;
  line-height: 1;
  margin: 0;
}
```

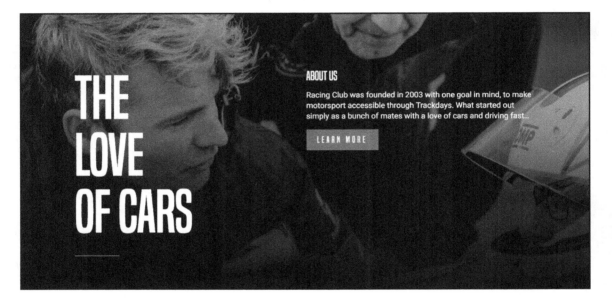

The final CSS code for the ABOUT US section is as follows:

```css
/* ABOUT US SECTION */

#about-us {
  width: 100%;
  background-image: url(../img/about-us-bg.jpg);
  background-repeat: no-repeat;
  background-size: cover;
  padding: 120px 0;
  color: white;
}

#about-us .container {
  display: flex;
  align-items: top;
```

```css
}

.about-us-title {
  width: 50%;
}

.about-us-title h3 {
  font-family: 'built_titling', Helvetica, sans-serif;
  font-weight: 400;
  font-size: 120px;
  line-height: 1;
  letter-spacing: -1px;
  margin: 0;
}

.about-us-title h3::after {
  content: "";
  display: block;
  background: #BF0000;
  width: 90px;
  height: 2px;
  margin-top: 30px;
}

.about-us-desc {
  width: 50%;
}

.about-us-desc h4 {
  font-family: 'built_titling', Helvetica, sans-serif;
  font-weight: 400;
  font-size: 26px;
  line-height: 1;
  margin: 0;
}

/* END ABOUT US SECTION */
```

Adding the Partner section

Let's go through this section efficiently, as we did with the last one.

Look at the following:

This section contains only a title, two images, text, and a button. We'll need to create a block inside our usual container (as shown in orange).

HTML:

```
<section id="partners">
</section>
```

Start with our `section` tag and `id`, which we name `partners`:

```
<section id="partners">
  <div class="container">
  </div>
</section>
```

As usual, we'll need our div `"container"` to maintain our structure:

```
<section id="partners">
  <div class="container">
    <div class="partners-container">
    </div>
  </div>
</section>
```

Inside, we create another container, `"partners-container"`:

```
<section id="partners">
  <div class="container">
    <div class="partners-container">

      <h2>Partners</h2>

      <div class="partners-inner">

        <div class="partner">
          <img src="img/partner1.png" srcset="img/partner1.png 1x,
img/partner1@2x.png 2x">
          <p>Advan Neova Cup</p>
        </div>

        <div class="partner">
          <img src="img/partner2.png" srcset="img/partner2.png 1x,
img/partner2@2x.png 2x">
          <p>JDM Style Tuning</p>
        </div>

      </div>

      <button type="button" name="button" class="btn-primary">Become a
partner</button>
    </div>
  </div>
</section>
```

Inside our `"partners-container"` div we do the following:

- We put our title into an h2
- We also created another div `"partners-inner"` to hold our two partners images
- Inside this `partner-inners` div, we have our single partner div with an image and a text each
- We also added a button, outside of `partners-inner` but inside `"partners-container"`

Our CSS will look like this:

```
#partners {
  background-color: black;
  color: white;
  text-align: center;
  padding: 50px 0px;
}
```

Here are some explanation of the code:

1. The background is `black`; since in the design, we have a black background
2. We can put the `color:white;` in the parent element so all elements inside will have the same property
3. We can do the same for `text-align:center;`
4. We also added some padding to the top and bottom

```
.partners-container {
  max-width: 400px;
  margin: 0 auto;
}
```

We added a `max-width` and `margin: 0 auto;` to center our `partners-container`. To align anything with the `margin: auto` method, you always need to define a width to the element:

```
.partners-container h2 {
  font-family: 'built_titling', Helvetica, sans-serif;
  font-weight: 400;
  font-size: 60px;
}
```

Also, add the following CSS:

```
.partners-inner {
  display: flex;
  margin: 30px 0px;
}

.partners-inner .partner {
  width: 50%;
}
```

To be able to use `display:flex;`, we'll need to set the `width` for the child elements.

You're done for the **PARTNERS** section; let's save it and take a look:

Our final CSS code for the **PARTNERS** section is as follows:

```
/* PARTNERS SECTION */

#partners {
  background-color: black;
  color: white;
  text-align: center;
  padding: 50px 0px;
}

.partners-container {
  max-width: 400px;
  margin: 0 auto;
}

.partners-container h2 {
  font-family: 'built_titling', Helvetica, sans-serif;
  font-weight: 400;
  font-size: 60px;
  line-height: 1;
```

```
}

.partners-inner {
  display: flex;
  margin: 30px 0px;
}

.partners-inner .partner {
  width: 50%;
}

/* END PARTNERS SECTION */
```

All done! Let's move to the final step, the footer!

Adding the footer section

In this section, we will be working on the footer section.

The footer is basically the same as the header, so to facilitate the coding, we will simply copy and paste the code from our header and change a few things:

```
<header>
  <a id="logo" href="/"><img src="img/logo.png" srcset="img/logo.png 1x,
img/logo@2x.png 2x"></a>
  <ul class="main-nav">
    <li><a href="upcoming.html">Upcoming events</a></li>
    <li><a href="past.html">Past events</a></li>
    <li><a href="faq.html">FAQ</a></li>
    <li><a href="about.html">About us</a></li>
    <li><a href="blog.html">Blog</a></li>
    <li><a href="contact.html">Contact</a></li>
  </ul>
  <ul class="right-nav">
    <li><a href="login.html">Login</a></li>
    <li><a href="#"><iframe
src="https://www.facebook.com/plugins/like.php?href=http%3A%2F%2Ffacebook.c
om%2Fphilippehongcreative&width=51&layout=button&action=like&size=small&sho
w_faces=false&share=false&height=65&appId=235448876515718" width="51"
```

```
height="20" style="border:none;overflow:hidden" scrolling="no"
frameborder="0" allowTransparency="true"></iframe></a></li>
    </ul>
</header>
```

Here are the things that we need to change:

- Change the <header> tag to a <footer> tag
- Add a .container div inside our footer as it follows the grid
- Change our logo image to "logo-footer.png"

This is the final HTML:

```
<footer>
    <div class="container">
        <a id="logo" href="/"><img src="img/logo-footer.png" srcset="img/logo-
footer.png 1x, img/logo-footer@2x.png 2x"></a>
        <ul class="main-nav">
            <li><a href="upcoming.html">Upcoming events</a></li>
            <li><a href="past.html">Past events</a></li>
            <li><a href="faq.html">FAQ</a></li>
            <li><a href="about.html">About us</a></li>
            <li><a href="blog.html">Blog</a></li>
            <li><a href="contact.html">Contact</a></li>
        </ul>
        <ul class="right-nav">
            <li><a href="login.html">Login</a></li>
            <li><a href="#"><iframe
src="https://www.facebook.com/plugins/like.php?href=http%3A%2F%2Ffacebook.c
om%2Fphilippehongcreative&width=51&layout=button&action=like&size=small&sho
w_faces=false&share=false&height=65&appId=235448876515718" width="51"
height="20" style="border:none;overflow:hidden" scrolling="no"
frameborder="0" allowTransparency="true"></iframe></a></li>
        </ul>
    </div>
</footer>
```

Let's jump to the CSS. We're first going to target our footer:

```
footer {
  background: black;
  color: white;
}
```

We're calling the `footer` without any dot or # because we're calling the tag by itself. It also means that every other `footer` tag will be selected. So, we need to make sure that we'll only select the tag `footer` for the `footer` element.

We add a background black like it is in the design but also add a `color:white` at the parent level. We're lazy, we don't want to add every time.

```
footer .container {
  display: flex;
  height: 120px;
}
```

This is getting interesting; we now have targeted the `.container` inside the `footer` and changed its property to `flex`, so we can display those elements inline.

We're not going to specify the width for each child element because we want them to take as much space as they would naturally take.

For the final touch, we'll add some padding to the logo to align it with the menu:

```
footer .logo {
  padding-top: 20px;
}

footer .main-nav li, footer .right-nav li {
  list-style-type: none;
  display: inline-block;
}

footer .main-nav li a, footer .right-nav li a {
  color: white;
  text-decoration: none;
  font-family: 'built_titling', Helvetica, sans-serif;
  font-weight: 200;
  font-size: 20px;
  letter-spacing: 4px;
  padding: 0px 15px;
}
```

We also took some styling from the `header` and copied it here:

We have our footer done now!

Here's the final CSS code:

```
/* FOOTER SECTION */

footer {
  background: black;
  color: white;
}

footer .container {
  display: flex;
  height: 120px;
}

footer .logo {
  padding-top: 20px;
}

footer .main-nav li, footer .right-nav li {
  list-style-type: none;
  display: inline-block;
}

footer .main-nav li a, footer .right-nav li a {
  color: white;
  text-decoration: none;
  font-family: 'built_titling', Helvetica, sans-serif;
  font-weight: 200;
  font-size: 20px;
  letter-spacing: 4px;
  padding: 0px 15px;
}

/* END FOOTER SECTION */
```

Summary

To summarize what we've done so far: We've created one web page from scratch also used HTML Boilerplate to kick-start our project. We've learned plenty of CSS techniques, and in particular about CSS flexbox, which can be very useful

For the next chapter, we'll tackle the responsive side of the CSS and also add some interactivity to our website. Let's jump into it!

8
Making Our Website Responsive

In Chapter 4, *Responsive Versus Adaptive Design,* you learned the difference between responsive design and adaptive design. The first one is a lot easier to implement, and the latter is targeted to the end user.

This chapter will cover the following:

- What are media queries?
- Opening the browser inspector
- The difference between desktop first and mobile first
- Introducing to jQuery
- How to make our website responsive for every device and screen size

What are media queries?

Responsive design can be accomplished using *media queries*. How does this work? Think of media queries as a condition that you apply to your CSS. You tell the browser to add or remove certain CSS rules depending on the device or viewport size:

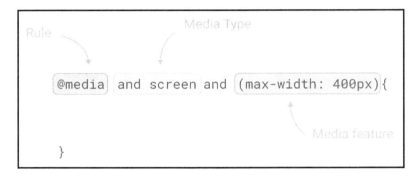

To apply those rules, we will need to use the CSS property @media, as follows:

```
/* Mobile Styles */
@media only screen and (max-width: 400px) {
  body {
    background-color: #F09A9D; /* Red */
  }
}
```

@media only screen and (max-width: 400px) means that if the screen/viewport size is fewer than or equal to 400px, then we apply this CSS.

There are a few different types of properties you can add to media and target a different type of device.

For example, you can target especially the iPhone 4 with the following code:

```
@media only screen
  and (min-device-width: 320px)
  and (max-device-width: 480px)
  and (-webkit-min-device-pixel-ratio: 2)
  and (orientation: portrait) {

}
```

This translates as the following:

```
and (min-device-width: 320px)
and (max-device-width: 480px)
```

The preceding code means any devices with a size greater than or equal to 320px and fewer than or equal to 480px:

```
and (-webkit-min-device-pixel-ratio: 2)
```

The following code targets any device with the pixel ratio or density of 2:

```
and (orientation: portrait)
```

The preceding code will target only devices with a portrait orientation.

Now that we have covered the basics of media queries, let's put this into practice with our project.

Opening the inspector

First, to be able to test our website's responsiveness, there is a tool available in Chrome that is very useful. To access it, you can go to **View | Developer | Developer Tools**:

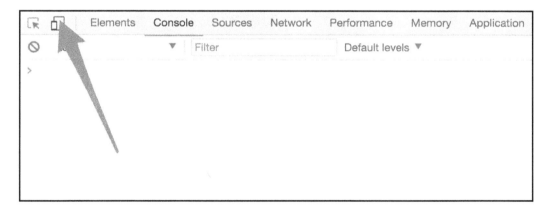

To use this tool, click on the second icon on the top left

Now, you can select any device you want to test with, as follows:

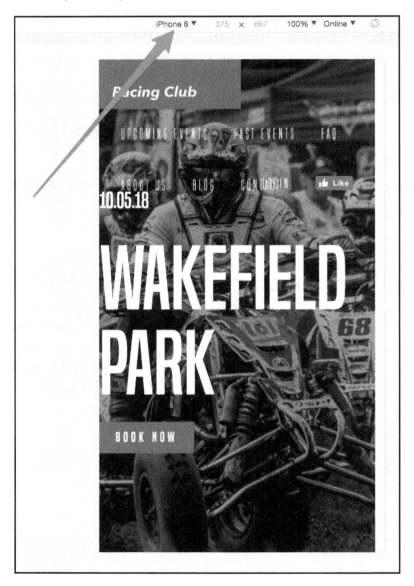

You can also see that the code of the entire page is displayed on the right-hand side:

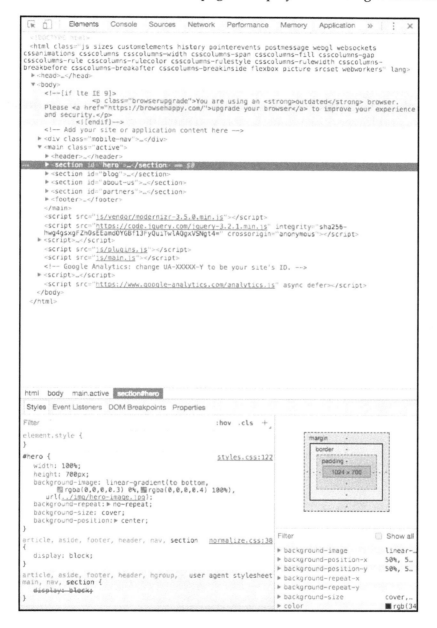

The Google Chrome Inspector

This is very useful, because it allows you to try different CSS properties before putting in your code or to check whether your CSS works. You can have a quick try and play around with it.

Desktop first

Depending on the design process you started with, but in general, you would start with the desktop design, and lower down to mobile. If you started your design with a mobile-first process, you'll have to start on a mobile and then upgrade to the desktop.

So, the initial CSS is for desktop, so what we have to consider now is what conditions we want to apply to the CSS.

The devices we want to target are as follows:

- Desktop (by default)
- Tablet (viewport size fewer than or equal to 1,024px)
- Large mobile (viewport size fewer than or equal to 768px)
- Small mobile (viewport size fewer than or equal to 400px)

This is an example of how you can separate the different breakpoints. You can definitely change it according to your needs.

So, this is how it looks in CSS:

```css
/* Tablet Styles */
@media only screen and (max-width: 1024px) {
}

/* Large Mobile Styles */
@media only screen and (max-width: 768px) {
}

/* Small Mobile Styles */
@media only screen and (max-width: 400px) {
}
```

Now that we have our breakpoint ready, let's start making our website responsive.

Designing the menu

In this section, we will take a look at how to hide the desktop menu and show a hamburger icon instead when working on mobiles or tablets:

The design of the mobile view

If we click on the icon, a menu opens on the right-hand side:

Menu opened on mobile

To do that, we will first need to hide the menu on the mobile version and the tablet version.

At the end of the header section in our CSS, add the following code:

```
/* Tablet Styles */
@media only screen and (max-width: 1024px) {
  header {
    display: none;
  }
}
```

Now we want to show the `hamburger-menu` on mobile. We will need to create a `div` tag in HTML and show it only on a mobile, with CSS:

```
<div class="hamburger-menu">
    <img src="img/hambuger-icon.svg">
</div>
```

We will place this just before the ending of our header tag `</header>`.

In CSS, we will need to hide the hamburger in desktop view and show it only on mobile view:

```
.hamburger-menu {
  display: none;
}
/* Tablet Styles */
@media only screen and (max-width: 1024px) {
  header .main-nav, header .right-nav {
    display: none;
  }
  .hamburger-menu {
    display: block;
  }
}
```

Let's save and take a look:

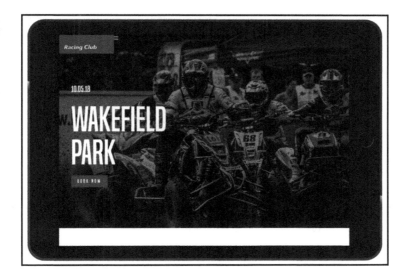

If you want to add a fancy frame to your tablet view, then click on the three dots in the right-hand corner and click on **Show device frame**.

We can see that the hamburger icon shows up, but we need to place it correctly:

```
.hamburger-menu {
    display: none;
    position: absolute;
    right: 15px;
    top: 15px;
}
```

Don't forget that we only change the `display` property with our media queries, so the rules we apply here will apply to the the mobile version.

Now we have to create another menu that shows up only on mobile version, and when the user clicks on the hamburger menu, the entire page will move to the left:

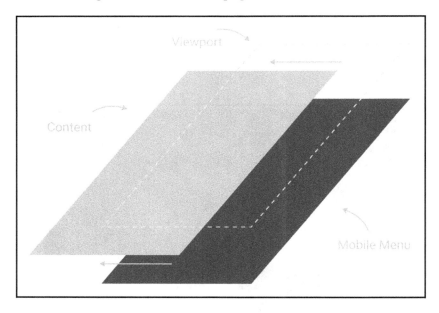

A diagram that shows the different layers of the content and the mobile nav

To be able to move the entire page, we will need to create an HTML tag and put our content inside it. We'll create a tag called `<main>` and put the content we created inside (from `header` to `footer`).

Now, in CSS, we will first need to add a new section for our `main` tag:

```
/* MAIN SECTION */

main {
}

/* END MAIN SECTION */
```

Now, to ensure that this element will be the parent element, we will need to make this element in a `position: relative;` so that every element with a `position: absolute;` will now relate to this one:

```
main {
  position: relative;
}
```

We'll also add a `background-color: white;` to make sure that it has the same background `white` as the default `white`:

```
main {
  position: relative;
  background-color: white;
}
```

Now, to move our `main` tag, we'll use the "`left:-200px`" CSS property:

```
main {
  position: relative;
  background-color: white;
  left:-200px;
}
```

This will move our element horizontally by −200px, that is, 200px to the left. Now, let's save and take a look:

Main container moved to the left by 250px

For our mobile menu, let's create another `div` with the `"mobile-nav"` class, but we will put it outside of the `<main>` tag:

```
<div class="mobile-nav">
</div>
<main>
    <header>
      ...
```

In `.mobile-nav`, let's recreate our `nav` (including `.main-nav` and `.right-nav` lists):

```
<div class="mobile-nav">
        <ul>
          <li><a href="upcoming.html">Upcoming events</a></li>
          <li><a href="past.html">Past events</a></li>
          <li><a href="faq.html">FAQ</a></li>
          <li><a href="about.html">About us</a></li>
          <li><a href="blog.html">Blog</a></li>
          <li><a href="contact.html">Contact</a></li>
          <li><a href="login.html">Login</a></li>
          <li><a href="#"><iframe
```

```
src="https://www.facebook.com/plugins/like.php?href=http%3A%2F%2Ffacebook.c
om%2Fphilippehongcreative&width=51&layout=button&action=like&size=small&sho
w_faces=false&share=false&height=65&appId=235448876515718" width="51"
height="20" style="border:none;overflow:hidden" scrolling="no"
frameborder="0" allowTransparency="true"></iframe></a></li>
          </ul>
        </div>
```

In our CSS file, let's make sure that you hide our .mobile-nav in desktop view:

```
/* MOBILE MAVIGATION */

.mobile-nav {
  display: none;
}

/* Tablet Styles */
@media only screen and (max-width: 1024px) {
  .mobile-nav {
    display: block;
  }
}

/* END MOBILE NAVIGATION */
```

Let's add some customization:

```
.mobile-nav {
  display: none;
  position: fixed;
  background-color: #1F1F1F;
  width: 200px;
  height: 100%;
  right: 0;
  top: 0;
}
```

- `position: fixed;`: As we want the menu to stay fixed on the back while we move the <main> container
- `background-color: #1F1F1F;`: The color picked from the design
- `width: 200px;` and `height: 100%;`: As we want the dimension to be slightly lower than the minimum width of a mobile, which is 320px. 200px seems good, and, of course, we want the height to be 100%, to take the entire space vertically

- `right: 0;` and `top: 0;`: Specify the position from the viewport

iPad View (1,024px)

Let's finish the customization of the menu:

```
.mobile-nav ul {
  margin: 0;
  padding: 25px;
}

.mobile-nav ul li {
  list-style-type: none;
  margin-bottom: 10px;
}

.mobile-nav ul li a {
  color: white;
  text-decoration: none;
  font-family: 'built_titling', Helvetica, sans-serif;
  font-weight: 200;
  font-size: 20px;
  letter-spacing: 4px;
}
```

Let's save and take a look at how it looks:

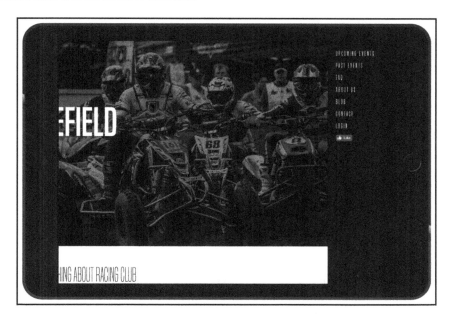

iPad View (1,024px)

Now let's return the `<main>` container to its initial position:

```
main {
  position: relative;
  background-color: white;
  left: 0px;
}
```

This is when the fun starts; we'll create a function in JS to animate the `<main>` container when the user clicks on the hamburger menu.

To make that happen, we will add a class to the `<main>` tag when the user clicks on the hamburger menu. This class called `active` will have the following value:

```
main.active {
  left: -200px;
}
```

So, if we add an `active` class to the `<main>` element, the container will move to the left as we specified.

Now let's remove it and get started with the JS.

To kick-start any project, the best way for any beginner is to start with jQuery. What is jQuery?

What is jQuery?

> *jQuery is a fast and concise JavaScript Library that simplifies HTML document traversing, event handling, animating, and Ajax interactions for rapid web development.*

-Official jQuery website

jQuery is not a language in itself; it is a JavaScript framework that helps to code JavaScript more easily and efficiently. The good points of jQuery are as follows:

- It simplifies JavaScript syntax
- It has fixed most of the issues that JavaScript will have between each web browser
- It makes deployment safer across all platforms
- It's easy for a beginner to understand
- It has many libraries and a big community

To use jQuery, we'll just need to link a script to our HTML, but, fortunately, with HTML boilerplate, jQuery is already integrated. The following is the line in our HTML that calls the URL and downloads the jQuery file:

```
<script src="https://code.jquery.com/jquery-3.2.1.min.js"
integrity="sha256-hwg4gsxgFZhOsEEamdOYGBf13FyQuiTwlAQgxVSNgt4="
crossorigin="anonymous"></script>
```

jQuery syntax

We will now have a look at the jQuery syntax. The following syntax is an example of a jQuery and JavaScript code that changes the background of the body:

jQuery
```
$('body').css('background', '#fff');
```

Javascript
```
function changeBackgroundColor(color) {
    document.body.style.background = color;
}
onload="changeBackgroundColor('white');"
```

You can see the big difference between them.

The basic syntax of jQuery is very simple:

```
$(selector).action();
```

1. The $ sign starts any jQuery action
2. The (selector) is used to query (or find) HTML elements, by ID or class like in CSS (# or .)
3. action() is the action to be performed on the element(s)
4. The semicolon (;) is used to close the action

For example, to add a class in jQuery, we can use the jQuery action .addClass:

```
$('main').addClass('active');
```

To make this happen, we will need to create a JS file beforehand and write all our JS code in there. However, we can use the one created by HTML boilerplate located in our js folder, called main.js.

To call jQuery and say that we need to do those actions, we will need to add the following code:

```
$(document).ready(function(){

    // jQuery methods go here...

});
```

This is to prevent any jQuery code from running before the document has finished loading.

Now, to test whether our jQuery is correctly linked with our HTML file, a quick thing we can do is to show an alert when the page loads.

To do so, we can use the JavaScript `alert` action:

```
$(document).ready(function(){

    alert("Hello world");

});
```

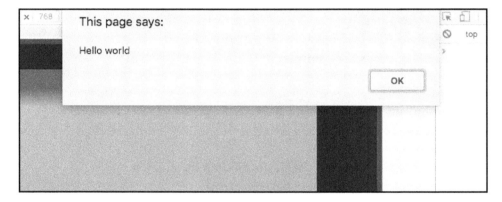

Our alert action is properly working

We can remove the `alert` action and add the little code we created earlier:

```
$(document).ready(function(){

    $('main').addClass('active');

});
```

Let's save and check whether everything works:

This shows the class on the Inspector

Indeed, we have our class `active` right from the start.

To change this action to when the user clicks on the menu, we will need to use the jQuery action, `click`:

```
$('.hamburger-menu').click();
```

We can define this, but this will not do anything, as we need to define the action when the icon is clicked. To do so, we will need to set a `function` inside. A function is a set of actions that you can set and is followed by an open and a closed curly bracket:

```
$('.hamburger-menu').click(function(){
});
```

Now, inside the `function`, we will add the `addClass` action:

```
$('.hamburger-menu').click(function(){
    $('main').addClass('active');
});
```

Now save your JS file and refresh the page. As you click on the `hamburger-menu`, the container moves to the left. Well done! We have our first step. However, now we want to close the menu and move the container back.

We can add this:

```
$('main').click(function(){
    $('main').removeClass('active');
});
```

However, this won't work, as it will always try to remove the class `active` as `<main>` is the parent of `.hamburger-menu`. To solve that, we will need to tell the script to stop the click `event` from bubbling up when we click on the trigger. This means that it will never reach the `<main>` level and won't trigger the `.removeClass()` method. To do so, we will need to add a way to track the click event and tell it not to bubble up:

```
$('.hamburger-menu').click(function(event){
    event.stopPropagation();
    $('main').addClass('active');
});
```

You can now check your menu. It's working properly as expected, but when you click on the `.hamburger-menu` itself, it doesn't do anything. This is because we didn't tell it to do anything.

We will need to make the `<main>` return to its initial position when we click on the hamburger-menu. However, right now, we have only set it to add a class `active` to `<main>`.

We need to configure a way to remove the class only if <main> has an active on it. To do so, we will need to apply a condition. To apply a condition in jQuery, we will simply need to use the condition if and else inside a function:

```
$('.hamburger-menu').click(function(event){
    event.stopPropagation();
    if (condition){
    } else {
    }
});
```

So, the action we want is as follows:

- If <main> has the class active, remove the class active
- If <main> doesn't have the class active, add the class active

To check whether an element has a class, we can use the jQuery action hasClass, as follows:

```
$('.hamburger-menu').click(function(event){
    event.stopPropagation();
    if ($('main').hasClass('active')){
        $('main').removeClass('active');
    } else {
        $('main').addClass('active');
    }
});
```

Now save your JS document. Our JS is working perfectly, but if you have a tendency to be a perfectionist, adding some animation won't kill you. We can add some transition to the container to add some smoothness to the animation:

```
main {
    position: relative;
    background-color: white;
    left: 0px;
    transition: all 0.2s ease-in-out;
}
```

The transition will only work on the element that is moving, which is, in this case, the <main> element.

Our responsive is finally done; let's move to the hero section.

Making the hero section responsive

Let's check how responsive our hero is at the moment:

iPad view and iPhone 8 view

As we see, there is nothing to change in the iPad view; however, for the iPhone view, it lacks padding and the title seems a bit too big.

The way I can see to fix this without too much code is to add some padding to the container, the container we have implemented in every section:

```
.container {
  max-width: 940px;
  margin: 0 auto;
}

/* Tablet Styles */
@media only screen and (max-width: 1024px) {
  .container {
    padding: 0px 15px;
  }
}
```

We will add some padding from the tablet breakpoint, so it will affect all lower breakpoints too.

Let's now fix our the title. This will be straightforward; we will just need to find our `.hero-title` class and add some media queries:

```
/* Large Mobile Styles */
@media only screen and (max-width: 768px) {
  .hero-text .hero-title {
    font-size: 90px;
  }
}
```

That's it! You can always change the value as you wish, as well.

Making the Blog section responsive

This **Blog** section is based on a three-column grid, and it works pretty well on desktops and tablets; however, on a mobile, it shrinks a bit too much, so we'll need to change the three columns to two columns (and one column for a small mobile):

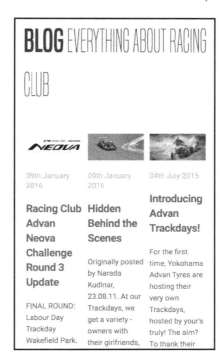

Mobile view of the Blog section

To change the width of the column, let's head to the `.blog-post` class we created and change the value of the width to `50%` on a large mobile breakpoint:

```css
.blog-post {
  width: 33.33%;
  padding: 0 5px;
  box-sizing: border-box;
  margin-bottom: 30px;
}

/* Large Mobile Styles */
@media only screen and (max-width: 768px) {
  .blog-post {
    width: 50%;
  }
}

/* Small Mobile Styles */
@media only screen and (max-width: 400px) {
  .blog-post {
    width: 100%;
  }
}
```

This will make sure that the content will still be readable, regardless of the device it will be appearing on.

Also, the title seems a bit big as well. We can reduce the `font-size` by `40px` when in mobile view:

```css
#blog h2 {
  font-family: 'built_titling', Helvetica, sans-serif;
  font-weight: 200;
  font-size: 60px;
}
```

```
/* Small Mobile Styles */
@media only screen and (max-width: 400px) {
  #blog h2 {
    font-size: 40px;
  }
}
```

The preceding code will look like this:

The view of the different breakpoints of the Blog section

Making the ABOUT US section responsive

The **ABOUT US** section looks fine on the iPad view but starts to become a bit squishy on a mobile:

Mobile view of the About Us Section

To fix this issue, we will need to change the width value to 100% on the mobile breakpoint:

```
.about-us-title {
  width: 50%;
}

/* Small Mobile Styles */
@media only screen and (max-width: 400px) {
  .about-us-title {
    width: 100%;
  }
```

```
}

.about-us-desc {
  width: 50%;
}

/* Small Mobile Styles */
@media only screen and (max-width: 400px) {
  .about-us-desc {
    width: 100%;
  }
}
```

Also, we will change the orientation of the flexbox by adding the CSS property, `flex-orientation: column`. By default, this value is `row`, but you also have the ability to change the order by having the `row-reverse` value, the same for the `column` value with `column-reverse`:

```
/* Small Mobile Styles */
@media only screen and (max-width: 400px) {
  #about-us .container {
    flex-direction: column;
  }
}
```

The design looks good, but the text is still a bit too close to the title; let's fix this by adding a margin:

```
/* Small Mobile Styles */
@media only screen and (max-width: 400px) {
  .about-us-desc {
    width: 100%;
    margin-top: 50px;
  }
}
```

Now, save and check:

The ABOUT US responsive layout

Making the footer section responsive

The last part is the `footer`, and, for most websites, it's just a list of links. It's usually displayed it as a simple vertical list; it's not as sophisticated as the header menu we created.

First, we will need to remove the height value we set in the `footer`; to do that, we can simply replace it with the `auto` value:

```
/* Small Mobile Styles */
@media only screen and (max-width: 768px) {
  footer .container {
    height: auto;
  }
}
```

We also need to display the links in a vertical way by setting the direction of the flexbox, as we saw earlier:

```
/* Small Mobile Styles */
@media only screen and (max-width: 768px) {
  footer .container {
    flex-direction: column;
    height: auto;
  }
}
```

The next step will be to change the value of the display we set on our `<li>`:

```
footer .main-nav li, footer .right-nav li {
  list-style-type: none;
  display: inline-block;
}

/* Small Mobile Styles */
@media only screen and (max-width: 768px) {
  footer .main-nav li, footer .right-nav li {
    display: block;
  }
}
```

Also, we need to remove the padding we set on the `<a>` tag:

```
/* Small Mobile Styles */
@media only screen and (max-width: 768px) {
  footer .main-nav li a, footer .right-nav li a {
    padding: 0px;
  }
}
```

Finally, we will need to remove the default padding from the `<ul>`:

```
/* Small Mobile Styles */
@media only screen and (max-width: 768px) {
  footer .container ul {
    padding: 0;
  }
}
```

Now we're all done.

Summary

That was quite a condensed chapter, I hope you're still following all this! Now that we have covered how to make our website responsive with media queries, and also with a quick introduction to jQuery, we can now move on to the next chapter. In our next chapter, we will move deeper into CSS and jQuery by adding some interaction and adding some dynamic content to your website. We'll discuss pseudo-class in CSS, how to use plugins on our website, and how to collect information through an API. I can't wait to show you this!

Adding Interaction and Dynamic Content

9

I find this part of building a website to be the most fun and enjoyable. Adding interaction and dynamic content will bring life to our website and add a personal touch to it.

In this chapter, we will:

- Start by learning the basics of **pseudo-class** in CSS, with a few examples of hover and active states
- Learn how to create a CSS animation from scratch
- Add some dynamic content by connecting to an API and importing some content to display on our website

Let's get started!

CSS pseudo-classes

A pseudo-class is used to define a special state of an element. For example, when you hover or when you click on a button, a state can be activated.

We're going to learn two easy pseudo-classes for the moment, the most common ones. You can easily add and activate other pseudo-classes when you know how to use them:

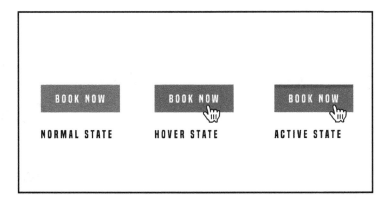

Different pseudo-classes

The two pseudo-classes are hover and active. The hover state is used when you hover over an element with the mouse. It's useful to show that the element is clickable. The active state, on the other hand, is used when you click on an element.

To use these pseudo-classes, you simply have to call them with a colon ::

```
.element:hover {
    // Display something
}

.element:active {
    // Display something
}
```

For the first example, we'll add some styling when hovering over the links in the menu. We want to add an underline to the link when hovering it. To do that, it will be better for us to be able to target every single <a> with a class. But if we look at our HTML, we have many different classes for each navigation. What we'll do is add a common class to each nav so we can call it with CSS easily.

We have the class .main-nav and .right-nav on the header and footer. What we'll do is add a common class .nav to each of those classes:

```
<ul class="nav main-nav">
            <li><a href="upcoming.html">Upcoming events</a></li>
            <li><a href="past.html">Past events</a></li>
```

```
            <li><a href="faq.html">FAQ</a></li>
            <li><a href="about.html">About us</a></li>
            <li><a href="blog.html">Blog</a></li>
            <li><a href="contact.html">Contact</a></li>
        </ul>
        <ul class="nav right-nav">
            <li><a href="login.html">Login</a></li>
            <li><a href="#"><iframe
src="https://www.facebook.com/plugins/like.php?href=http%3A%2F%2Ffacebook.c
om%2Fphilippehongcreative&width=51&layout=button&action=like&size=small&sho
w_faces=false&share=false&height=65&appId=235448876515718" width="51"
height="20" style="border:none;overflow:hidden" scrolling="no"
frameborder="0" allowTransparency="true"></iframe></a></li>
        </ul>
```

Now, we have to target the link inside the nav. The link is the element `<a>` as we saw earlier. To target it, we will call in CSS as follows:

```
.nav li a {
  // CSS
}
```

This will target every `<a>` in every `<li>` that is a child of every `.nav`.

Let's add the pseudo-class `:hover` :

```
.nav li a:hover {
  // CSS
}
```

To add an underline under a link, we can use the CSS property `text-decoration:underline;`:

```
.nav li a:hover {
  text-decoration: underline;
}
```

Now let's add some styling for the button as well.

For every button, we have the class `.btn-primary`, so, with the same process as before, we'll add the pseudo-class `hover`:

```
.btn-primary:hover {
  background: #A3171B;
}
```

What we did here is to change the background color of the button when hovering over it. Let's now add an `active` state:

```
.btn-primary:active {
  box-shadow: inset 0px 8px 4px rgba(0, 0, 0, 0.25);
}
```

This will add an inner-shadow to the button when clicking on it.

To add an extra touch, we can add a `transition` to make the action smoother. Don't forget, a `transition` has to be added in the normal state, not on the pseudo-classes:

```
.btn-primary {
  display: inline-block;
  font-family: 'built_titling', Helvetica, sans-serif;
  font-weight: 400;
  font-size: 18px;
  letter-spacing: 4.5px;
  background: #BF0000;
  color: white;
  padding: 12px 22px;
  border: none;
  outline: none;
  transition: all 0.3s ease;
}
```

Voila! Pretty easy. There are plenty of pseudo-classes in CSS. We'll go through some more but you can already have a play around. Here's a list of pseudo-classes in CSS: `https://www.w3schools.com/css/css_pseudo_classes.asp`.

The next step is to build a sticky navigation! We'll combine some jQuery and CSS and build a navigation that sticks to the top when the user scrolls the page. Exciting times!

Sticky navigation

What we want to do is make the navigation stick to the top when we scroll passed the **Blog** section, as shown in the following screenshot:

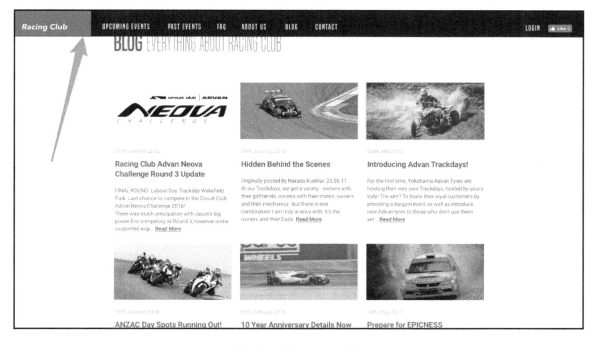

The sticky navigation we want to build.

To make this happen, we'll add an extra class with jQuery on the header. This extra class will make the navigation stick to the top and make the navigation background dark. Let's first create this extra class:

```
header.sticky {
}
```

We need to be careful here as we didn't separate the class with space, which means it's when the header has also the class `sticky`.

To this class, we will add the following properties:

```
header.sticky {
  position: fixed;
  top: 0;
  background-color: #212121;
  background-image: none;
}
```

Let's break that down:

- We use `position: fixed;` as we want to make the navigation stick to the top. `position: fixed` will position the element relative to the browser window.
- `top: 0;` tells us it will stick to the top.
- `background-color:` sets a solid background color.
- `background-image: none;` removes the gradient.

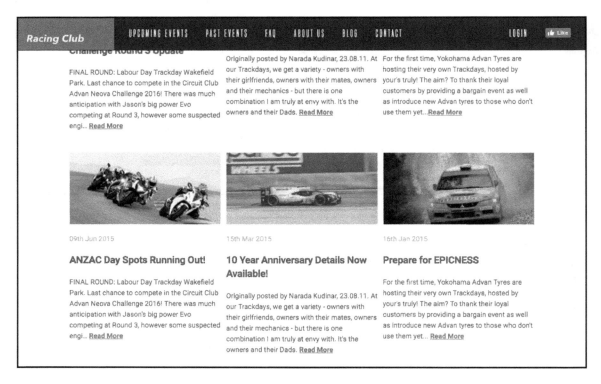

Sticky header on the Blog section

We have our CSS class `.sticky` ready to go. Now we have to create our jQuery function to make this happen.

JS Plugin: Waypoints

We're going to use a plugin that triggers an action when scrolled to an element. The plugin is called *Waypoints* and can be downloaded from this link: `http://imakewebthings.com/waypoints/`:

Waypoints website.

Simply click on the **Download** button to download the files. In the files that you have downloaded, only one file will be necessary. Go to the `lib` folder and look for `jquery.waypoints.min`. Copy this file and paste it to our `Web Project` folder, specifically in our `js | vendor` folder.

Once pasted, we need to link it to our HTML page. To do so, go to our HTML file before the closing tag `</body>`. You'll see a bunch of scripts that were already linked previously for our jQuery file. Before the last file `main.js`, simply add the following:

```
<script src="js/vendor/jquery.waypoints.min.js"></script>
```

`main.js` should be the last file in the list because it contains all our personal JS functions and needs to read by the browser last.

Every plugin has a different way to be used. The best way is to read the document provided by the author of the plugin. Here, I'll explain to you the easiest way to use this plugin.

To use `.waypoint` with jQuery, we can call it with the following:

```
$('elementToTrigger').waypoint(function(direction){
    /* JS code */
});
```

Here are some explanations:

- `elementToTrigger` will be the element we want the plugin to watch and trigger the action when the user scroll passes the element. In this case, it will be `#blog`.
- `direction`: this argument will serve to detect whether the user is scrolling down or up the page.

Let's head to our `main.js` and create our own `JS code`:

```
$('#blog').waypoint(function(direction) {

});
```

Now what we want is to do an action when the user scrolls `down` and scrolls past the **Blog** section, but also do another action when the user scrolls up and leaves the blog section.

To do that, we'll need to use a condition, as we saw earlier:

```
$('#blog').waypoint(function(direction) {
    if (direction == 'down') {
    } else {
    }
});
```

`direction == 'down'` means the direction of the scroll is equal to `down`.

Now what we want to do is to add the class `sticky` when the user scrolls `down` and passes the blog section, and remove the same class when the latter leaves it:

```
$('#blog').waypoint(function(direction) {
    if (direction == 'down') {
      $('header').addClass('sticky');
    } else {
      $('header').removeClass('sticky');
    }
});
```

Let's save and see how it works:

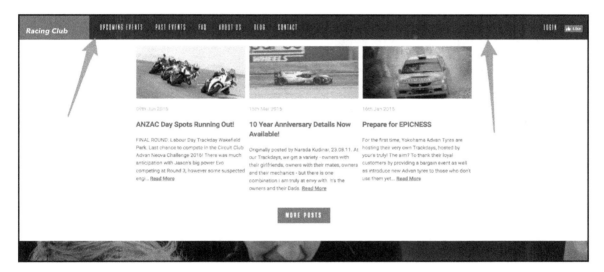

Our sticky header.

It works perfectly, but the header appears instantly, with no animation whatsoever. Let's try to make it a bit smoother. To add a bit a transition, we'll use, in this example, CSS animation.

CSS animation

CSS animation allows for the creation of animation without JS or Flash, with keyframes and every CSS property. It offers more advantages than a simple transition.

To create a CSS animation, you need to create a keyframe:

```
/* The animation code */
@keyframes example {
    from {background-color: red; }
    to {background-color: yellow; }
}
```

`from` means at the start of the animation, while `to` means at the end of the animation.

You can also be more precise with the timeframe by setting the percentage:

```
/* The animation code */
@keyframes example {
    0% {background-color: red; }
    25% {background-color: yellow; }
    50% {background-color: blue; }
    100% {background-color: green; }
}
```

To trigger the animation, you need to call it in the specific div with the CSS properties:

```
animation-name: example;
animation-duration: 4s;
```

For our header navigation, the keyframe would be:

```
/* The animation code */
@keyframes sticky-animation {
    from {transform: translateY(-90px); }
    to {transform: translateY(0px); }
}
```

`transform:` is a new type of position in CSS that allows you to move an element in a 2D or 3D environment. With `translateY`, we're moving the element in the *Y-axis*. Also, we named the keyframes `sticky-animation`:

```
header.sticky {
  position: fixed;
  top: 0;
  background-color: #212121;
  background-image: none;
  animation-name: sticky-animation;
  animation-duration: 0.3s;
}
```

The last part will be to call the animation in the class `.sticky`, with a duration of `0.3s`.

We now have a sticky navigation that works perfectly, with a cool animation!

Adding a dynamic Instagram feed

The end goal here is to be able to implement your own Instagram feed by connecting to the Instagram API and pulling out information from them.

From a design point of view, we want to show a feed of our latest photo from Instagram after our footer, with a hover effect of opacity when you move your mouse over it.

It should look something like this:

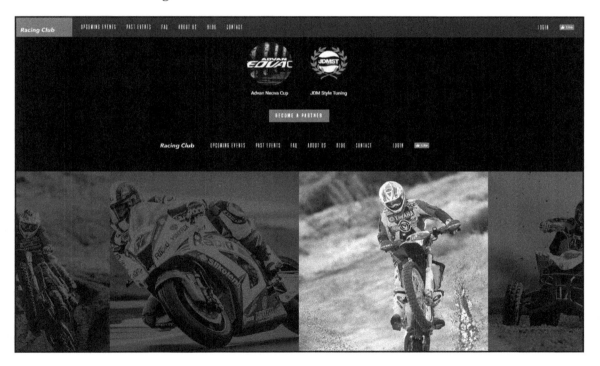

The final design of our Instagram feed

To achieve that, first, we need to have an Instagram account. If you already have one, you can use your own. Otherwise, I've created an account for the exercise:

Our awesome Instagram feed

Installing Instafeed.js

I have, beforehand, uploaded a couple of images of racing. The next step is to install a plugin called `Instafeed.js`. Let's go to the website to download it: `http://instafeedjs.com/`:

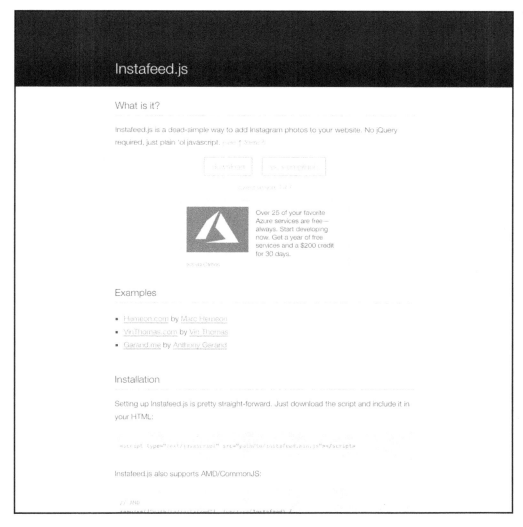

Instafeed.js home page

Right click on **download** and click on **Save link As...**. Place the file in the `vendor` folder, located in the `js` folder in our `Web Project`.

For each plugin, the installation is quite similar each time. All the installation process is generally detailed on the website itself. Let's have a look at Instafeed's documentation.

Setting up `Instafeed.js` is pretty straight-forward. Just download the script and include it in your HTML:

```
<script type="text/javascript" src="path/to/instafeed.min.js"></script>
```

First, we need to call the `js` file we initially placed in our `vendor` folder:

```
<script src="js/vendor/modernizr-3.5.0.min.js"></script>
<script src="https://code.jquery.com/jquery-3.2.1.min.js"
integrity="sha256-hwg4gsxgFZhOsEEamdOYGBf13FyQuiTwlAQgxVSNgt4="
crossorigin="anonymous"></script>
<script>window.jQuery || document.write('<script
src="js/vendor/jquery-3.2.1.min.js"><\/script>')</script>
<script src="js/vendor/jquery.waypoints.min.js"></script>
<script src="js/vendor/instafeed.min.js"></script>
<script src="js/plugins.js"></script>
<script src="js/main.js"></script>
```

Place it after the Waypoints plugin we previously installed.

Now, if we look thoroughly at the documents, we can find the section we need.

Getting images from your user account

To fetch images specifically from your account, set the `get` and `userId` options:

```
<script type="text/javascript">
    var userFeed = new Instafeed({
        get: 'user',
        userId: 'YOUR_USER_ID',
        accessToken: 'YOUR_ACCESS_TOKEN'
    });
    userFeed.run();
</script>
```

The next step is to find the userID and TokenAccess. If you don't want to create an Instagram account and want to use the one I created beforehand, you can go straight to the section titled **Displaying the feed**.

Finding our userID and TokenAccess

The information we need to find is the `userID` and the `accessToken`. To get the `userID`, we need our Instagram username. Instagram didn't really make it easy to find our `userID`. Fortunately, there are plenty of people who created an easy way to find it. You can easily find a way by googling *How to find Instagram userID*, but we'll go straight to the point. Just head to this website `https://codeofaninja.com/tools/find-instagram-user-id` and fill the input with your Instagram username:

The Find Instagram User ID website

After clicking on **Find Instagram ID**, you'll get something like this with your `User ID`:

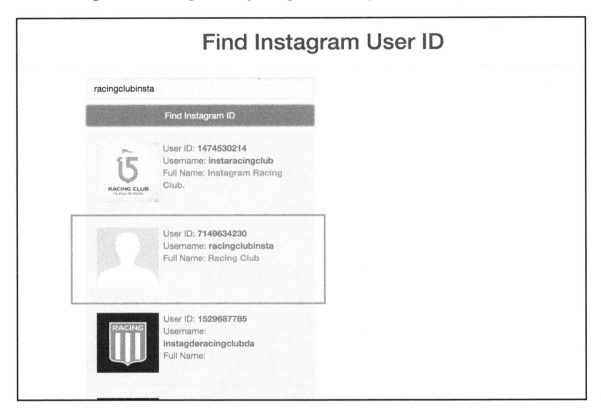

Our userID

Now let's head to our `main.js` and copy/paste the example of code showed in the `instafeedjs` documentation. After our `Sticky Nav` code, paste the code:

```
// INSTAGRAM

    var userFeed = new Instafeed({
        get: 'user',
        userId: 'YOUR_USER_ID',
        accessToken: 'YOUR_ACCESS_TOKEN'
    });
    userFeed.run();
```

Just copy and paste the `userID` we got from the website, replacing `'YOUR_USER_ID'`:

```
// INSTAGRAM

    var userFeed = new Instafeed({
        get: 'user',
        userId: '7149634230',
        accessToken: 'YOUR_ACCESS_TOKEN'
    });
    userFeed.run();
```

It's not done; we still need our access token. This will be a bit more complicated.

Getting our access token

Instagram didn't really make it easy to find the access token either. Usually, it would take quite a bit of time to generate our access token, but we'll use a tool to help us get it. Let's head to `http://instagram.pixelunion.net/` and click on **Generate Access Token**.

This site will generate for us a token access with one click, the only thing we need is to authorize the website to access our account:

 **Pixel Union**　　　　　　　　Themes　Support　Blog

 Get Your Instagram Access Token

In order to display your Instagram photos on your own website, you are required to provide an Instagram Access Token. You can do this by clicking the generator button below. After clicking, you'll be prompted by Instagram to authorize Pixel Union to access your Instagram photos, and you may need to enter your Instagram login credentials.

You'll be brought right back here and, if all went well, your Instagram Access Token will be ready for you. Copy and paste this access token into the correct field. Remember to keep your access token private and never paste it in a location where others might can access it.

FREQUENTLY ASKED QUESTIONS

What's an Instagram Access Token?

The Instagram Access Token is a long string of characters unique to your account that grants other applications access to your Instagram feed.

Why do I need a token?

Without the token, your website will be unable to talk to the Instagram servers. The token provides a secure way for a website to ask Instagram's permission to access your profile and display its images.

The Pixel Union website

Click on **Generate Token Access**; it should direct you to the Instagram *Authorization* page:

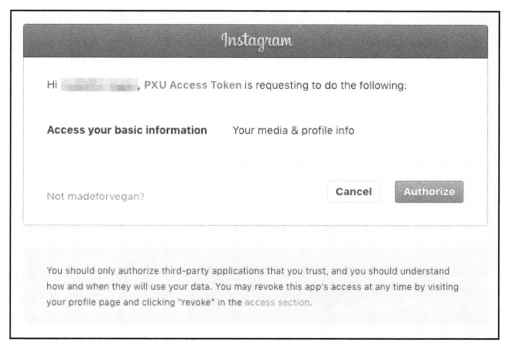

Instagram Authorization page

Once done, you can copy paste the code provided by them:

It worked!

Use this token in the appropriate field on your website or blog, and you should have a working Instagram widget.

7149634230.1677ed0.45cf9bad017c431ba5365cc84797...

If you're having problems using your token, get in contact with the service that set up the theme or template you're using for your website. If you're using a Pixel Union theme, our customer support team would be happy to help!

© 2018 Pixel Union

Shopify Themes • BigCommerce Themes • Ecommerce Apps

Pixel Union Access Token Code

Let's copy/paste the last piece of the puzzle in our `main.js` code:

```
// INSTAGRAM

var userFeed = new Instafeed({
    get: 'user',
    userId: '7149634230',
    accessToken: '7149634230.1677ed0.45cf9bad017c431ba5365cc847977db7',
});
userFeed.run();
```

Save the `main.js`. The next step is to fill the HTML with photos of our Instagram feed.

Displaying the feed

How does the Instafeed plugin work to display our feed? It will look for the `<div id="instafeed"></div>` and fill it with linked thumbnails.

Let's head to the end of our HTML file, after our `<footer>` tag, and add `<div id="instafeed"></div>`:

```html
<footer>
          <div class="container">
            <a class="logo" href="/"><img src="img/logo-footer.png"
srcset="img/logo-footer.png 1x, img/logo-footer@2x.png 2x"></a>
            <ul class="nav main-nav">
              <li><a href="upcoming.html">Upcoming events</a></li>
              <li><a href="past.html">Past events</a></li>
              <li><a href="faq.html">FAQ</a></li>
              <li><a href="about.html">About us</a></li>
              <li><a href="blog.html">Blog</a></li>
              <li><a href="contact.html">Contact</a></li>
            </ul>
            <ul class="nav right-nav">
              <li><a href="login.html">Login</a></li>
              <li><a href="#"><iframe
src="https://www.facebook.com/plugins/like.php?href=http%3A%2F%2Ffacebook.c
om%2Fphilippehongcreative&width=51&layout=button&action=like&size=small&sho
w_faces=false&share=false&height=65&appId=235448876515718" width="51"
height="20" style="border:none;overflow:hidden" scrolling="no"
frameborder="0" allowTransparency="true"></iframe></a></li>
          </ul>
        </div>
      </footer>
      <div id="instafeed"></div>
```

Let's save and see how it looks:

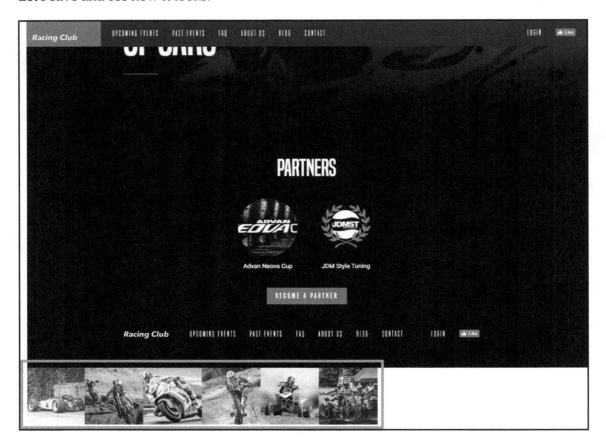

Our Instagram feed indeed appears, but we can't leave it like this. Let's customize our feed and add a bit of CSS to make it pretty.

The first thing we're going to do is to get larger images from our feed. By default, Instafeed gets the smallest size of thumbnails from Instagram. To get bigger thumbnails, we can read the documentation, and find the following information:

In the *standard option* provided by Instafeed, we can see that we have the option to choose between three types of resolution from the **thumbnail**s with the attribute `resolution`:

```
o  most-liked - Highest # of likes to lowest.
o  least-liked - Lowest # likes to highest.
o  most-commented - Highest # of comments to lowest.
o  least-commented - Lowest # of comments to highest.
o  random - Random order.
■  links - Wrap the images with a link to the photo on Instagram.
■  limit - Maximum number of images to add.
■  resolution - Size of the images to get. Available options are:
   o  thumbnail (default) - 150x150
   o  low_resolution - 306x306
   o  standard_resolution - 612x612
```

Instafeed documentation.

Let's choose the largest one. To add this option, we simply need to add an attribute to our JavaScript function:

```
// INSTAGRAM

var userFeed = new Instafeed({
    get: 'user',
    userId: '7149634230',
    accessToken: '7149634230.1677ed0.45cf9bad017c431ba5365cc847977db7',
    resolution: 'standard_resolution'
});
userFeed.run();
```

So, after `accessToken`, we can add the attribute `resolution`. Be sure to add a comma after the end of the attribute `accessToken` to mention that this is not the last property. The last attribute doesn't need a comma at the end.

Save and see what we have:

Website work in progress

Great, now it needs a bit of CSS to make this pretty. Before heading to the CSS, we need to check what HTML Instafeed generates for us, so we are able to call it in CSS. If you remember, we can inspect the HTML of an element in Google Chrome. We just have to right-click on it and click on **Inspect**:

Our Google Chrome inspector

We can see that Instafeed generates a `<a>` tag with an `<img>` inside. Pretty
straightforward.

Knowing that, let's go to our `styles.css` file, and write, after our `footer` section:

```css
/* INSTAFEED */

#instafeed {
  width: 100%;
  display: flex;
  justify-content: center;
  overflow: hidden;
  background: black;
}

#instafeed a {
  flex-grow: 1;
}
```

To explain, we use:

- `width: 100%;` because #instafeed is our container that holds everything. We want it to take the full width.
- `display: flex;` because we want to display the thumbnails horizontally side by side.
- `justify-content: center;` to place the content in the center.
- `overflow: hidden;` because we don't want the page to extend horizontally.
- `background: black;` because by default the background is white.

And, last, but not the least, the most important one:

- `flex-grow: 1;`: The remaining space in the `container` will be distributed equally to all children if all items have flex-grow set to 1. If one of the children has a value of 2 or more, the remaining space or more would take up twice as much space as the others.

Let's see how it looks now:

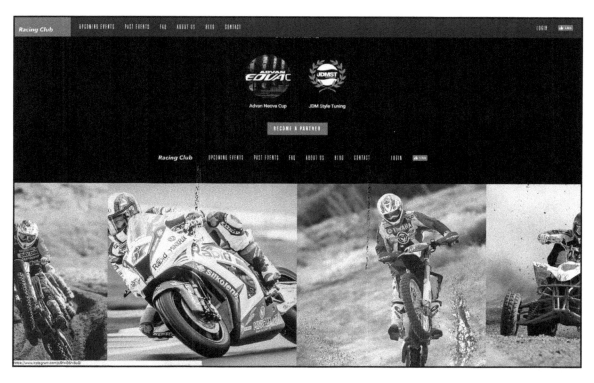

Website work in progress

Now, the last part is to add that opacity effect when hovering it. We'll play with opacity and pseudo-class :hover we learned just earlier:

```
#instafeed a {
  flex-grow: 1;
  opacity: 0.3;
}

#instafeed a:hover {
  opacity: 1;
}
```

Again, you only need to add the value you want to change in the pseudo-class; here, it is the opacity.

Let's also add some `transition`:

```
#instafeed a {
  flex-grow: 1;
  opacity: 0.3;
  transition: opacity 0.3 ease;
}
```

Let's save it and see:

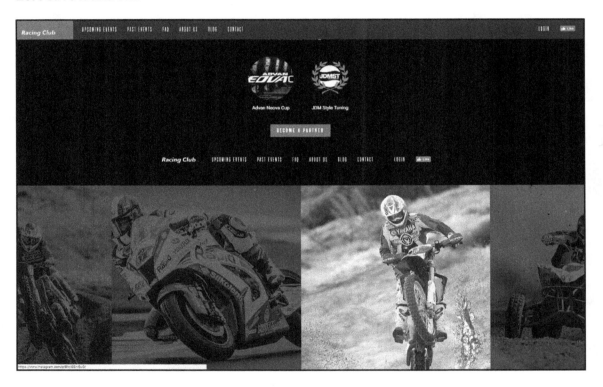

Website work in progress

Perfect, we did a great job so far. But if you're a perfectionist, as I am, you'll notice that on mobiles and tablets, the images are quite big. Let's add some quick responsive CSS and we can wrap this up:

```
/* Tablet Styles */
@media only screen and (max-width: 1024px) {
  #instafeed a img {
    max-width: 300px;
  }
}
```

```
}

/* Large Mobile Styles */
@media only screen and (max-width: 768px) {
  #instafeed a img {
    max-width: 200px;
  }
}

/* Small Mobile Styles */
@media only screen and (max-width: 400px) {
  #instafeed a img {
    max-width: 100px;
  }
}
```

What I did here is to change the image size on each breakpoint:

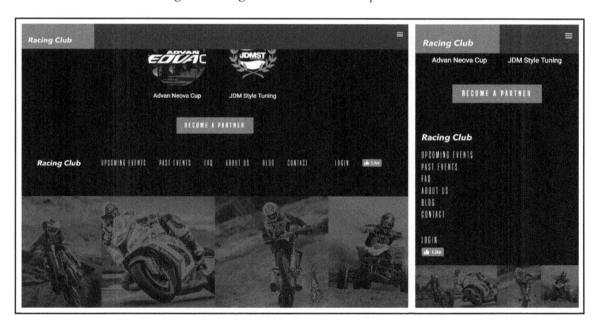

Tablet and mobile view of our Instagram Feed

We're now done with the interaction and dynamic content of our website.

Summary

Obviously, there are plenty of things you can do and add to your website. This has just been a little preview of what can be achieved very quickly. Again, your imagination and determination will be the only limit. Here's what we've covered in this chapter:

We've learned the CSS pseudo-class and how it can help with different animation. We've learned how to create animation with CSS `@keyframe`. We can now target elements with JQuery and add different functions to it. We've learned how to connect to an API and display information by using a plugin

A lot of exciting stuff in this chapter! In the next chapter, we will cover how to optimize our website and publish it!

Optimizing and Launching Our Website

10

Welcome to the last part of creating our website; we have come such a long way. Our website looks super great and has some cool animations. In this chapter, we will optimize our website by:

- Creating and implementing a favicon to our website
- Learning how to optimize our images
- Learning some SEO basics
- Going through how to publish our website online step by step

Let's get started!

Creating a favicon

Favicons are those little icons you see on browser tabs and on your bookmarks bar. They are part of the identity of any website and make users recognize your website:

Favicon of the Dribbble website

Don't skip this step. There is a very easy online tool to do this. We just need an image to serve as our icon, so let's do that for now. Let's go to `https://realfavicongenerator.net/`, which is the favicon generator. With this, we can create icons for browsers or even design them according to the different operating systems that it will run on. We just need to pick our image. In this case, we're going to use the logo provided in the assets folder, and find the image `Logo_Square.png`. Click **Select your Favicon picture** on the website and upload the logo.

Here's what we have:

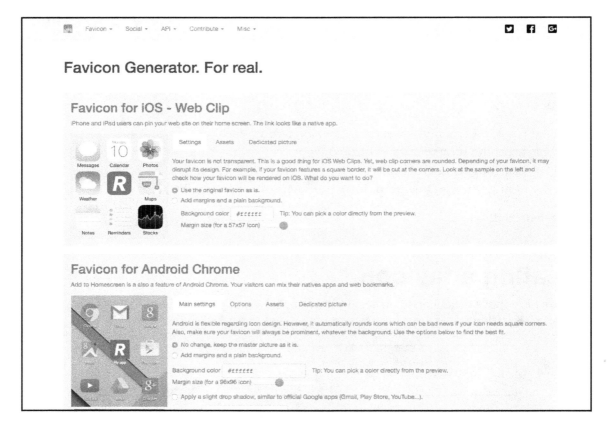

It provides us with a bunch of icons for iOS, Android, and Windows phones with some customization, but this is not really what matters. What really matters is what's at the bottom of the page:

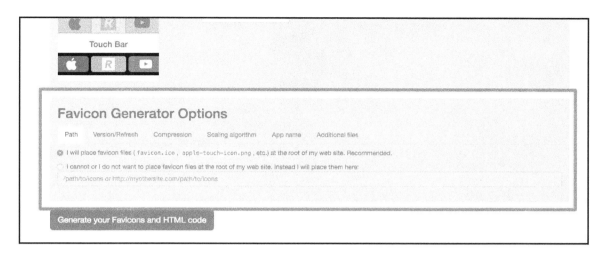

We will now click on the second option because we want to choose a path where we are going to put our icons since we don't want them in the root, in the main project folder. The website recommends that we put the favicon in the root, but we'll specify a different path, since there will be a lot of images and we want to keep it organized. Let's create a folder inside our `img` folder, and call it `icons`. Then, we'll edit the value in the input on the website and put `/img/icons` as the folder we just created. Now, let's generate the favicon! First, we need to click on *Generate your Favicons and HTML code*, which will take us to another page, and then we can click on the Favicon package to download it. There is also a code snippet provided, which we can copy and paste.

This code will be inserted into the `<head>` tag of our website, just after `<!-- Place favicon.ico in the root directory -->`.

You can remove the three lines of code provided by Boilerplate now:

```
<link rel="manifest" href="site.webmanifest">
<link rel="apple-touch-icon" href="icon.png">
<!-- Place favicon.ico in the root directory -->
```

Our `head` section should look like this now:

```
<head>
        <meta charset="utf-8">
        <meta http-equiv="x-ua-compatible" content="ie=edge">
        <title></title>
        <meta name="description" content="">
        <meta name="viewport" content="width=device-width, initial-
scale=1">
```

```
        <link rel="apple-touch-icon" sizes="180x180"
href="/img/icons/apple-touch-icon.png">
        <link rel="icon" type="image/png" sizes="32x32"
href="/img/icons/favicon-32x32.png">
        <link rel="icon" type="image/png" sizes="16x16"
href="/img/icons/favicon-16x16.png">
        <link rel="manifest" href="/img/icons/site.webmanifest">
        <link rel="mask-icon" href="/img/icons/safari-pinned-tab.svg"
color="#5bbad5">
        <link rel="shortcut icon" href="/img/icons/favicon.ico">
        <meta name="msapplication-TileColor" content="#da532c">
        <meta name="msapplication-config"
content="/img/icons/browserconfig.xml">
        <meta name="theme-color" content="#ffffff">

        <link href="https://fonts.googleapis.com/css?family=Roboto:400,700"
rel="stylesheet">
        <link rel="stylesheet" href="fonts/font.css"> <!-- Font face CSS
link -->
        <link rel="stylesheet" href="css/normalize.css">
        <link rel="stylesheet" href="css/animate.css">
        <link rel="stylesheet" href="css/main.css">
        <link rel="stylesheet" href="css/styles.css">
    </head>
```

The last step is to copy the files which we downloaded to our `icons` folder. Well done! Let's jump to the next section, where we will see how to optimize the performance of our website.

Site performance optimization

Nobody likes slow websites; we all know that. Besides that, page speed can have a real impact on your user's engagement, because nobody wants to wait for a website to load. We've added a few plugins and a lot of images. Now, let's start optimizing our website and make our users love our website even more by using some techniques for speeding up upload times. There are two very basic things we can do, which are to optimize heavy images and to minify CSS and jQuery code. Let's do that.

Optimizing images

The first thing we have to optimize is our images, and that is because images are usually by far the more heavy content of our webpage. Some of our images are quite heavy, such as our hero image, which is more than 480KB. All of these images, combined with when we download the website, take a long time. Imagine someone with a slow internet connection on a smartphone who is trying to download this site. This would take them forever. So, let's reduce the file sizes. As a first step, we can reduce the actual image size.

I use a tool called `TinyJPG` to compress heavy images. I find it more powerful than integrated optimization from Sketch or Photoshop:

Tinyjpg.com

What you have to do is just drag and drop the image you want to compress. Let's try this out with our `hero-image`, which has a size of 480KB:

hero-image.jpg after compression

Here, you can see that, after compressing `hero-image.jpg`, it is now almost half the size! Incredible, isn't it? Now what we have to do is compress as many files as we can to reduce their sizes.

Optimizing our code

Another thing that we can do is minify CSS and jQuery code. This basically reduces the size of the CSS and the jQuery files by removing unnecessary white space and optimizing that code. However, the minifying code makes it quite difficult for humans to read, so we should only minify code when we are ready to launch a website. One tool that I use is Minifier (`https://www.minifier.org/`). We can simply paste our code inside:

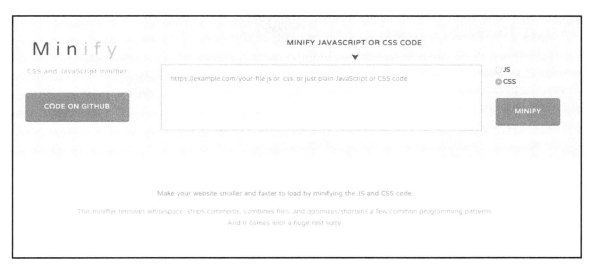

Minifier.org

This technique is actually more important when we have large amounts of code to compress; otherwise, we will not save as much space. In our case, we don't have that much code, so maybe it's not necessary to do this.

If you want to un-minify a code, there is another website for that: `http://unminify.com/`.

Now, let's move on to some very basic search engine optimization in the following section.

Basic SEO improvement

Search engine optimization (**SEO**) is a very hot topic. This is because it's so incredibly important that your website can be found by your users using a search engine, such as Google.

What is search engine optimization?

Basically, search engine optimization or SEO uses a couple of techniques that improve and promote a website to increase the number of visitors the site receives from search engines. There are many aspects to SEO, but we will just cover the very basic ones get our website search engine ready.

Meta description

First, and most importantly, we need a title for our website. This is the most important thing for SEO and users to understand the website.

At the top of your HTML, there is a `<title>` tag that we're going to fill. In this example, we'll add `Racing Club - Motor Racing Club for passionate`:

```
<title>Racing Club - Motor Racing Club for passionate</title>
```

Secondly, let's talk about the `meta description` tag. This tag is a short description of a website, and it's normally used to describe a website on the search result page, just as we can see here in this example of **Dribbble**'s website:

Shots - Dribbble - Dribbble
https://dribbble.com/ ▾
Shots from popular and up and coming designers in the **Dribbble** community, your best resource to discover and connect with designers worldwide.

Search result of the term "Dribbble"

```
<meta name="description" content="Shots from popular and up and coming
designers in the Dribbble community, your best resource to discover and
connect with designers worldwide." />
```

This text is not visible to visitors of the webpage itself, but it helps you advertise for your site, drawing users to your website from the search results. It is, therefore, an extremely important part of search marketing. We should craft a compelling meta description using important keywords, but with no more than 160 characters.

Now, let's do that for our webpage; there's nothing easier than that. We just use the `meta` tag with the `name="description"` attribute, and then the `content` attribute with the description we want. We want to add something about the Racing Club, so we'll put something like this: "A Racing Club by passionates to passionate. Monthly events in Australia-wide. Buy your ticket now.". In our HTML, we have a `meta` already pre-added, so we only need to put the description inside:

```
<meta name="description" content="A Racing Club by passionates to
passionate. Monthly events in Australia-wide. Buy your ticket now.">
```

You can see the line at the top of your HTML:

```
<meta charset="utf-8">
```

This is used to declare the character encoding of the website, but it doesn't include the ranking, so it has nothing to do with SEO. This is something that we should include in every website we make, though.

Valid HTML

We should always write valid HTML code. Valid HTML code is a code that follows the official HTML rules and has no bugs. Valid HTML is preferred by Google since it makes websites more likely to work on browsers we haven't tested. It looks more professional, and it's better for accessibility, making it easier for screen readers to read websites for blind users, for instance. There is an official tool for checking whether we have valid HTML code, which is called W3 markup validator (`https://validator.w3.org/`). We are going to use it to test our website. To do that, we just copy the entire code using command or *Ctrl + A*, and then copy it. On the website, validator.w3, we will use the **Validate by Direct Input** option and paste all our code here before clicking **Check**. It takes a little time, but it tells us that we have eight errors in our code.

In the Report, we can see a few recommendations:

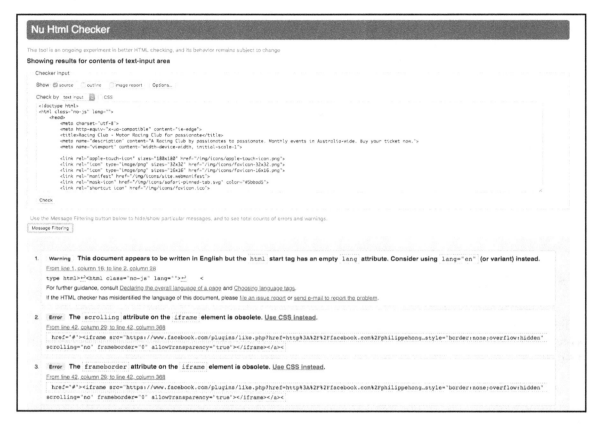

W3 validator report

One of the recommendations is that we should try to follow what the report advises us to do, but, again, you can still launch the website as it is.

At first, it says that:

This document appears to be written in English but the HTML start tag has an empty lang attribute. Consider using lang="en" (or variant) instead.

Indeed, it's recommended to specify the language of your website so that search engines can recognize it and be able to translate it if necessary. Let's add the en value (for English) in our lang attribute:

```
<html class="no-js" lang="en">
```

Secondly, it advises us to get rid of some attributes on the iframe that we implemented, but also to remove the <a> tag before the iframe. Let's do this.

Lastly, it says that:

An img element must have an alt attribute, except under certain conditions.

The `alt` attribute is the alternative attribute. It serves to describe the photo when it's loading or whether the browser couldn't render the image properly. It also serves for Google when searching for images, so it's very important.

Let's add an `alt` attribute to all our images, for example:

```
<img src="img/logo-footer.png" srcset="img/logo-footer.png 1x, img/logo-
footer@2x.png 2x" alt="Logo Racing Club">
```

Now let's check our code again:

Successful verification on W3 Markup Checker

Well done; our code is now validated!

Keywords

The next thing to think about is that *content is king*. It's very important that you have great content on your website, even if your website is one of the top search results. If your content is not great and your users don't want to read it, then it is not worth anything, even though you're so highly ranked. Also, keep providing new content if you can so that your visitors want to keep coming back for more. The next thing you need to do is place keywords strategically in your content. This is key to performing well in search ranking because keywords are what users actually use to find you. Be careful, though; don't overuse keywords, since search engines consider that as keyword spamming, and they may penalize you. Use keywords in a title, meta-description tag, headings, and links.

Links

Another important thing is to get other websites to link to you. These links are called backlinks and are like letters of recommendation for your website. Search engines rank websites based partially on the number and the quality of links that point to the site. This is a crucial factor to SEO, and therefore you should have a strategy to increase the quantity and quality of backlinks to your site. There is actually so much more information about SEO out there on the internet. If you're interested, check out some books or information on the internet; it's a passionate subject.

That's it for optimization. Let's move on to our next section, where we will learn how to launch our website on the internet.

Launching our website

Our website is now ready to be shared with the world. We have come such a long way, and now we are almost at the end. Launching our website is super easy to do. We just need to follow these three steps.

Buying a domain name

First, we need to choose and buy a domain name. For our website, that could be `www.racingclub.com`. Then, we need to buy web hosting; think of it as a folder on the internet where we'll put all our files. To ensure that our website runs smoothly, we need the right amount of bandwidth. That is the amount of data transfer we are allowed within a certain time period.

Once we have both of those things, we just need to upload our website to our web space, and then we are ready to go. There are many domain registration companies and web-hosting companies. Of course, I will not tell you which one you should choose. All I can tell you is that I have used `namecheap.com` to both register the domain name and buy web hosting. The service there was always great, but I can't tell you that it's the best web host out there because I have not tried any other server so far.

You can go to the *Namecheap* website and check whether your domain is available before you buy it. This is pretty easy and straightforward:

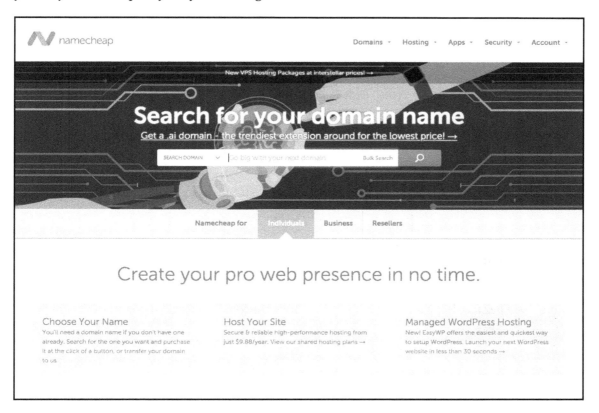

Once you have your domain, you need a host. I recommend getting the hosting and the domain with the same provider so it's easier to manage.

When purchasing your hosting, you can choose to use the domain you purchased or your own one:

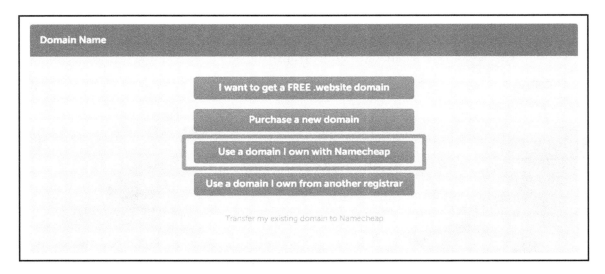

Buying hosting with Namecheap

Once you have bought your hosting and linked it to your domain, you'll receive a few emails confirming your purchase, but, more importantly, all the credentials for you to connect to your server as well as your **File Transfer Protocol** (**FTP**). This is a protocol used to transfer files to a server. To upload our files, we need a tool that uses this protocol. I always use *FileZilla*. Easy and open source, it does the job. The next step is to download FileZilla (`https://filezilla-project.org/`):

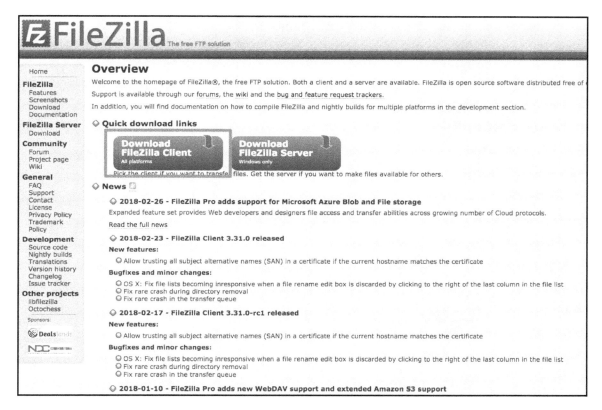

FileZilla website

Click on **Download FileZilla Client**, and install FileZilla properly.

Once you're on FileZilla, click on **File** | **Site Manager**:

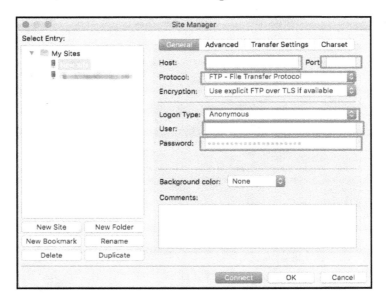

FileZilla new website

Now we need to add a new site, but we need to find the credentials Namecheap sent us. Go to your email and look for **SFTP Details**, which should look something like this:

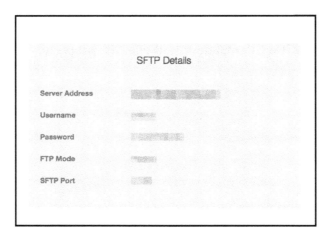

Namecheap SFTP credentials

Look at these descriptions of the SFTP details so that you put in the correct information:

- **Host**: This is the server address
- **Port**: This is the Port
- **Protocol**: Needs to be set in SFTP
- **Login Type**: Set to Normal
- **Username** and **Password**: Put accordingly

Click on **Connect**.

Now you'll see a bunch of folders, with every sort of name. Don't worry about them; look for `public_html`, since this will be your `public` folder. Once inside, you can delete the files set by default.

Now go to `Web Project` and select all the files that you with to drop into FileZilla. *Be careful;* all of the files, including hidden files, need to be uploaded. If you're in Windows, you don't need to worry about this, but for Mac users, hidden files are shown with a dot before the files. To show hidden files, simply use the shortcut *Shift + CMD + .* to show our hidden files:

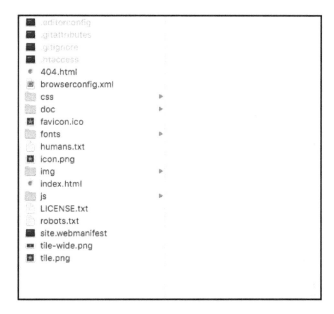

Showing hidden files in macOS

Now drag and drop all the files to FileZilla. It will automatically upload them to your server. Once this is done, your website is now officially online!

This will be different with every hosting provider, but generally, it is the same process. FileZilla is a great tool and can be used with every hosting if they're using FTP or SFTP to transfer files.

Google analytics

Now that our website is online, we can still work on it, because the launch is not the end of the story. The only thing you need to cover is site maintenance. This means that you should keep track of your website's success and monitor your users' behavior. How do we do this? We use a very powerful tool called Google Analytics. With this software, you will be able to monitor statistics like the number of visits your website receives, the amount of time your visitors stay, the average number of page views for each visitor, and many other useful statistics:

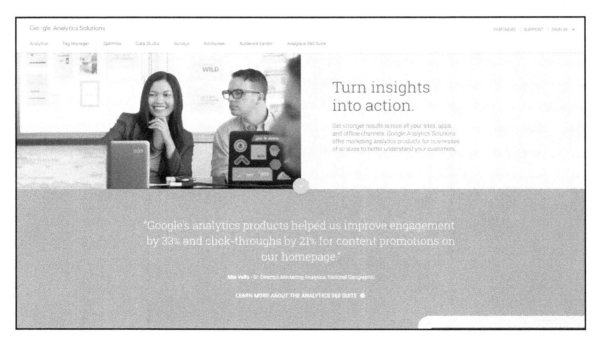

Google Analytics website

Then, using this data, you can make adjustments to the website to make it better. I will now install Google Analytics on the website I just uploaded to show you how easy it is. You need to start off by creating an account for Google Analytics, but that's easy if you already have a Google account. Once you have your Google Analytics account created, you need to create an account to get a tracking code:

New account in Google analytics

In our case, it's a website, and I will call this `Racing Club`. Then, we need the link this to our website. Type in all of the necessary information and hit **Get Tracking ID**:

Google Analytics tracking code

Google has now provided you with a code to paste into your website. It's a basic JavaScript code, so you can paste it after all the scripts.

In our HTML boilerplate, there is a spot left for our Google analytics code. Just replace the code with the code provided by Google:

```
<script src="js/vendor/modernizr-3.5.0.min.js"></script>
        <script src="https://code.jquery.com/jquery-3.2.1.min.js"
integrity="sha256-hwg4gsxgFZhOsEEamdOYGBf13FyQuiTwlAQgxVSNgt4="
crossorigin="anonymous"></script>
        <script>window.jQuery || document.write('<script
src="js/vendor/jquery-3.2.1.min.js"><\/script>')</script>
        <script src="js/vendor/jquery.waypoints.min.js"></script>
        <script src="js/vendor/instafeed.min.js"></script>
        <script src="js/plugins.js"></script>
        <script src="js/main.js"></script>

        <!-- Global site tag (gtag.js) - Google Analytics -->
        <script async src="https://www.googletagmanager.com/gtag/js?id=YOUR
GOOGLE ANALYTICS CODE"></script>
        <script>
          window.dataLayer = window.dataLayer || [];
          function gtag(){dataLayer.push(arguments);}
          gtag('js', new Date());
```

```
gtag('config', 'YOUR GOOGLE ANALYTICS CODE');
</script>
```

Now the final step is to upload the updated file to our server with FileZilla. Just drag and drop the `index.html` (don't forget to save!) and you're done!

This was a very quick introduction to Google Analytics, but the tool is very powerful and can be set up to track everything on your website. This was quite a long journey, but we did it. You can now actually open a web page on the internet and see the website that we created together. Now you are able to do all of this on your own. Amazing, isn't it?

Google Search Console

When everything is done, you can finalize your launch by telling Google to look at your website and to crawl it with their robot. To do this, we need to add our URL to the Google database, and we will do this by using their Google Search Console (`https://www.google.com/webmasters/tools/`):

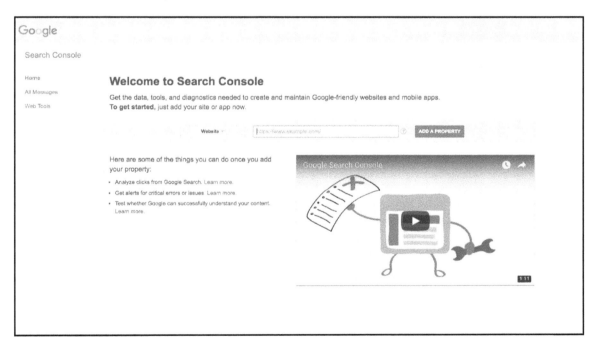

Google Search Console

Simply put in your domain name, verify that you own this domain, and you're all set.

Summary

Well done. We've covered quite a bit in this chapter. In this chapter, we've walked through the process of launching our website. From creating our favicon, compressing our images, minifying our CSS and JS files, we have also managed to validate our HTML with W3 Markup Validator. Followed by the purchase of our domain name and the upload of our files to our server. We finished the chapter by integrating Google Analytics and submitting our website to Google Search. It was a very condensed chapter we can say it!

In this next chapter, we will learn what Bootstrap is and why developers love it. We will also learn about its components, we will learn how to use Bootstrap Grid, and, finally, how Bootstrap uses Media Queries.

Let's jump to the next chapter!

11
What is Bootstrap?

Now that we know how to build a website from scratch, I want to introduce you to Bootstrap (`https://getbootstrap.com/`).

In this chapter, we will:

- Learn what Bootstrap is and why developers love it
- Go through the documentation of Bootstrap and understand how to use it
- Get our hands on the Famous Bootstrap Grid
- Understand how Bootstrap uses Media Queries

What is Bootstrap?

Bootstrap is an open source HTML, CSS, and JS library that helps you build websites and apps very easily. It is a library of components that you can reuse instead of re-creating every component over and over again. Bootstrap is responsive and mobile first; this is essentially what Bootstrap is all about, and why it has become so popular with web developers. Now, let's say the developers are creating different versions of their website for different devices; just by applying small amounts of code to the pages, the sites will be displayed correctly on any device, which saves time and additional cost.

There are major updates every couple of years. Bootstrap 2 was officially released in 2012, then was reasonably quickly replaced with Bootstrap 3, which was released in 2013. Then, of course, there came Bootstrap 4 in 2016. The more stable it becomes, the longer the gaps between the releases. Hopefully, it won't be too long before Bootstrap 5 arrives.

Bootstrap 4 is still very new, so a lot of developers are still using Bootstrap 3:

Bootstrap website

Within the framework, there are also a large number of elements and components that you can use within your sites or pages. Everything in the **Documentation** tab will be essential; it contains invaluable information that you can refer back to, and is where you want to go to learn about new elements or components:

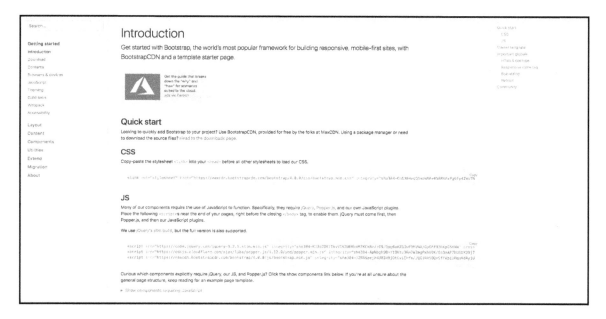

Bootstrap documentation

It starts with the introduction to Bootstrap and includes all the information you need to get started. Then, on the left-hand side, it provides all the sections and components. This is probably one of the most popular sections you will view as it contains all the different elements you can use within Bootstrap. So, essentially, this can help you build your pages.

There are also some examples or quick start examples that Bootstrap provides in the **Examples** tab. These are ideas for practicing or testing things out after you've completed this chapter, so you can put your new ideas into your own page and test out what you've learned throughout the chapter:

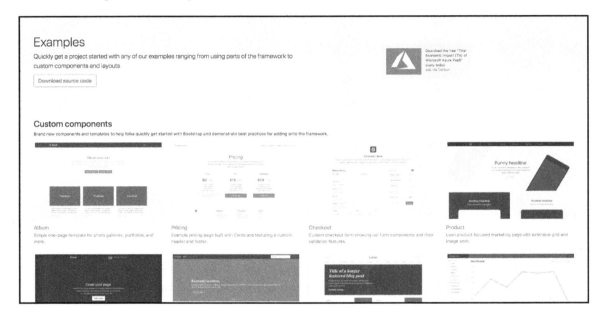

Bootstrap Examples.

It's worth bookmarking this page or coming back here in the future. Now, another essential section to keep an eye on is the Bootstrap blog; this is where all the updates are posted, no matter how big or small. So, it's ideal to keep an eye on it just in case some changes occur that may have an effect on your site.

So, in a nutshell, that's just a quick overview of the Bootstrap site. It's worth bookmarking the components page so you can quickly refer back to it in the future if you need to. Next, we're going to take a closer look at what those components are, and how we are going to use them.

Components

Let's have a look at our Bootstrap documentation (https://getbootstrap.com/docs/4.0/getting-started/introduction/), more specifically the **Component** section. This sits on the **Documentation** tab and contains a lot of the elements that you will use by coding your website with Bootstrap:

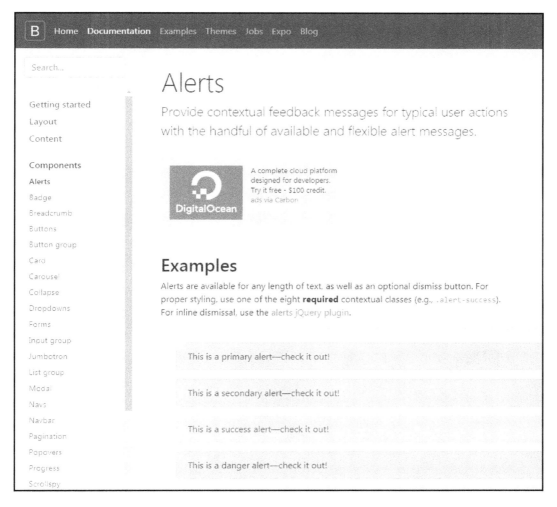

Bootstrap components

These are all listed in alphabetical order, so you can easily find what you need. For example, if we just have a look at the buttons, this provides all you need to know on getting started with buttons in Bootstrap. The default buttons have their own style classes; we can see here that there's primary, secondary, success, danger, warning, info, light, dark, and link:

Bootstrap buttons

To add any of these buttons to your page, you could use this code that's provided here, or if you wanted the outline of a button, for example, if we just scroll down, you can see that the outline buttons have their own class as well. You just need to add this code to add an outline button:

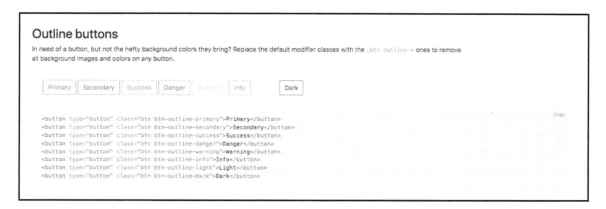

Bootstrap Outline buttons

If we just continue to scroll down, you can see that there are many different button options available. Of course, you can just add a standard button and start it yourself manually, but these examples are a great way to get up and running quickly with buttons on your page.

Now, obviously, buttons aren't that exciting; it's just an example of how much detail there is in Bootstrap and how much support there is when coding in Bootstrap. Let's have a look at another example, such as forms. We have all our form contents on the right side here. Let's just click on **Inline forms**, for example; we can see all the information describing the inline form option, but also the code that you need to add to your page:

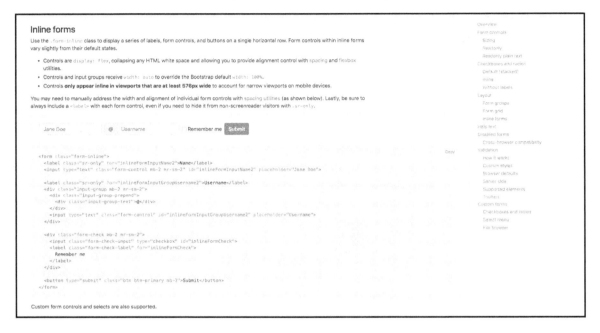

Inline forms

If you choose another one, Navbar, for example, this shows all the different options you can use when adding navigation bars to your page. It starts with the basics then states **the Navbar requires a Navbar class** and that its fluid by default. This just means that they stretch the entire width of the page. Then, it goes on to describe the different elements of the Navbar, including adding your brand, the different color schemes, and how to make your Navbar responsive. There is a lot of information to help make sure you can quickly get up and running if you need to. Feel free to have a look around these components if you want. It's certainly worth bookmarking this page too for future use.

We'll obviously go into more detail as we start to build our page. Next, we are going to move on and have a look at the Bootstrap **Grid system**.

Bootstrap Grid system

One of the main reasons why Bootstrap is so popular is due to the responsive nature of the framework. Now, Bootstrap is built on a grid system, and it's based on a set of 12 columns. If you just jump into the **Documentation** on the Bootstrap website, then into the **layout** section, and then to the **Grid** section, we can take a closer look:

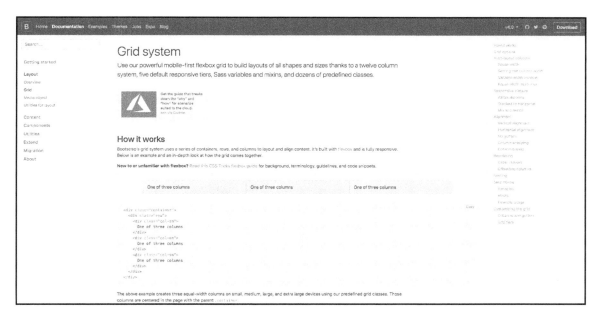

Bootstrap Grid

Bootstrap contains three different components; they are the columns, containers, and rows. Essentially, the containers hold the content, the rows align the content, and the columns dictate how the content is split along that row. Don't worry too much if that doesn't make sense because you've got no experience of the grid system; it will all become clear as you work your way through the chapter and get hands-on experience. To give the best example of what the grid system is all about, we can take a look at the **Responsive classes** section on the following page. I feel this gives the best explanation of what the **Grid system** is all about: The Bootstrap:

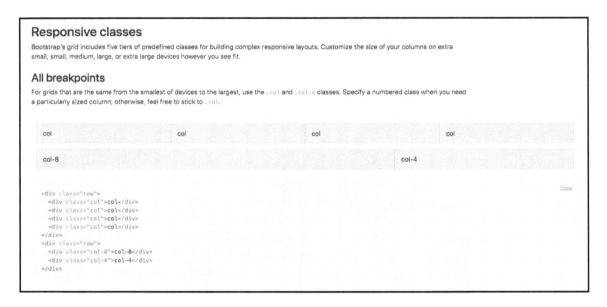

Responsive class in Bootstrap

There are five tiers of predefined classes for building complex responsive layouts. In this example, we can see that the new `col` class is being used. This means that in this row, we have essentially four columns along the same row, and each element is taking up a specific number of columns along the 12 column row.

In the first case, each element is taking up three columns along the 12 column row, as three goes into 12 four times. This layout will also be the same on all devices, from extra small all the way up to extra large. You can also define the number of columns you want to take up along the row if you wanted, which is in this example in the second row.

So, the first bit of content will take up 8 columns, and the next will take up 4. Again, that will fill the entire 12 columns along the row, no matter what the screen size is. Bootstrap is so popular because of its responsive nature and the fact that certain elements are stacked on the smaller devices and they are aligned along the row on the larger devices. To do that, we simply need to define the device size within our column class:

Stacked to horizontal

Using a single set of .col-sm-* classes, you can create a basic grid system that starts out stacked before becoming horizontal with at the small breakpoint (sm).

col-sm-8		col-sm-4
col-sm	col-sm	col-sm

Copy

```
<div class="row">
  <div class="col-sm-8">col-sm-8</div>
  <div class="col-sm-4">col-sm-4</div>
</div>
<div class="row">
  <div class="col-sm">col-sm</div>
  <div class="col-sm">col-sm</div>
  <div class="col-sm">col-sm</div>
</div>
```

Responsive feature

In this next example you can see that by using the sm class, or the small class, the content is similar, as we have 8 and 4 on the top, then the next row is switched into three sections. However, on the live example of both the content would actually stack on the smaller devices, and when the breakpoint hits anything above the smaller devices, it will display along the row. There is a lot more information on the **Grid system** within this page, however, as I mentioned, you'll soon get used to how it works as we work our way through the chapter.

I hope that explains the **Grid system** a little, but, as I said, you'll soon get the hang of it by working with it in the next chapter. Next up, we're going to have a look at Bootstrap media queries.

Media queries

One of the best things about Bootstrap is the fact that you can incorporate media queries into your CSS files, which essentially lets you start specific items or breakpoints and helps you target styles for specific devices. If you first head to the **Documentation** tab and then head to the **layout** section, then we just need to scroll down slightly to the **Responsive breakpoint** section. We can see our media queries here. We can see that the breakpoints are important as these are generally used as guidelines for the queries so you can determine which device you want a style for:

Responsive breakpoints

Since Bootstrap is developed to be mobile first, we use a handful of media queries to create sensible breakpoints for our layouts and interfaces. These breakpoints are mostly based on minimum viewport widths and allow us to scale up elements as the viewport changes.

Bootstrap primarily uses the following media query ranges—or breakpoints—in our source Sass files for our layout, grid system, and components.

```
// Extra small devices (portrait phones, less than 576px)
// No media query since this is the default in Bootstrap

// Small devices (landscape phones, 576px and up)
@media (min-width: 576px) { ... }

// Medium devices (tablets, 768px and up)
@media (min-width: 768px) { ... }

// Large devices (desktops, 992px and up)
@media (min-width: 992px) { ... }

// Extra large devices (large desktops, 1200px and up)
@media (min-width: 1200px) { ... }
```

Since we write our source CSS in Sass, all our media queries are available via Sass mixins:

```
@include media-breakpoint-up(xs) { ... }
@include media-breakpoint-up(sm) { ... }
@include media-breakpoint-up(md) { ... }
@include media-breakpoint-up(lg) { ... }
@include media-breakpoint-up(xl) { ... }

// Example usage:
@include media-breakpoint-up(sm) {
  .some-class {
    display: block;
  }
}
```

We occasionally use media queries that go in the other direction (the given screen size *or smaller*):

```
// Extra small devices (portrait phones, less than 576px)
@media (max-width: 575.98px) { ... }

// Small devices (landscape phones, less than 768px)
@media (max-width: 767.98px) { ... }
```

Responsive breakpoint

In this first section of code, we have the media queries for all the breakpoints except the extra small devices. This uses the `min-width` command. If we scroll down slightly we can see that we have all the breakpoints except for the extra large devices and these use the `max-width` command. The difference is that you tend to use the `min-width` option if you're designing for mobile first and the `max-width` if you're designing for desktop first:

```
We occasionally use media queries that go in the other direction (the given screen size or smaller):
                                                                                                      Copy
// Extra small devices (portrait phones, less than 576px)
@media (max-width: 575.98px) { ... }

// Small devices (landscape phones, less than 768px)
@media (max-width: 767.98px) { ... }

// Medium devices (tablets, less than 992px)
@media (max-width: 991.98px) { ... }

// Large devices (desktops, less than 1200px)
@media (max-width: 1199.98px) { ... }

// Extra large devices (large desktops)
// No media query since the extra-large breakpoint has no upper bound on its width
```

max-width command

Generally, I tend to use `max-width` and I tend to design for desktop first, however; it is good to have an understanding of both, just in case you need to design for mobile first as well.

That was a simple introduction to media queries; again, you get a better understanding of that as we go through the course, but I hope that explains things a little so you have a basic understanding when we actually get there.

Summary

The important points to remember in this chapter is that Bootstrap are like a library of components that developers can easily reuse. By knowing them (grid, components. media queries), you'll be able to achieve a lot compared to when you're building the website from scratch.

Next, we'll get on with designing our page with Bootstrap and learn, step by step, how to use it.

12
Building a Website with Bootstrap

We just saw how powerful Bootstrap can be. With an extensive list of components and elements we can reuse, it can make our development phase very easy, and that's why developers love it. In this chapter, we'll discuss how to build our website using the Bootstrap framework using the following steps:

- Learning how to set up Bootstrap in your project
- Creating and styling our Navigation bar
- Continuing with the hero section
- Creating and styling the Blog section
- Creating and styling the About section
- Finishing with the Footer

We'll start the project from scratch and create the same page we created before to compare our initial technique with the Bootstrap technique. Let's get started!

Installing Bootstrap

The first thing we will need to do is download Bootstrap. There are any ways to download it. Let's head to the download page to check it out. Click on the **Download** button on the homepage. Now you can take a look at the different methods of downloading the latest version of Bootstrap:

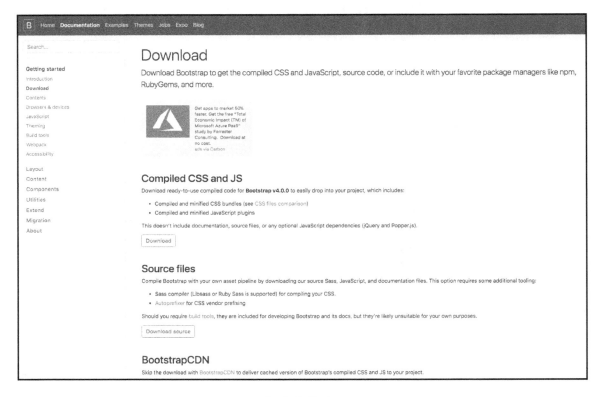

Downloading Bootstrap

The first method is to download the Compiled version of Bootstrap. Your version will depend on when you take this course, but always take the latest version of Bootstrap.

You can also download the source version of Bootstrap with all the files, but, most of the time, you'll only need the compiled files, because it's quicker and easier to get Bootstrap up and running.

If you scroll down a little bit, you would notice **BoostrapCDN**. Bootstrap also provides a **Content Delivery Network** (**CDN**) that will host the latest version of Bootstrap in a server, so you can paste only the URL without having to host the files on your server. It's pretty good, as your users will not have to download the files again, as it might have already downloaded the files by visiting another website using Bootstrap.

Setting up our project

To get started, let's create a folder called `Racing Club Bootstrap`. In Atom, we will open a new window, click on **Add Project Folder...**, and locate the `Racing Club Bootstrap`.

Inside, let's create our `index.html` file. Click on **Create New** (*Ctrl + N* or *Cmd + N*), and save it so that we can name the file `index.html`.

Once done, let's head to the Bootstrap website (`http://getbootstrap.com/docs/4.0/getting-started/introduction/`), specifically, the **Introduction** section.

In this section, Bootstrap provides you with a template to kick-start your project:

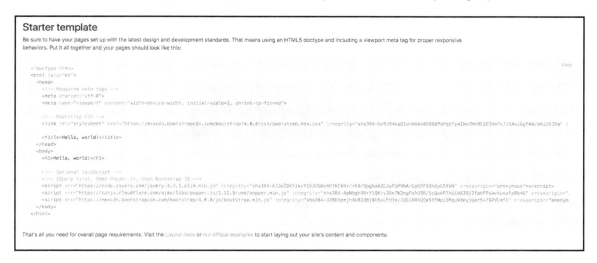

The Starter template

Copy the code provided and paste it into your `index.html` file. We can remove `<h1>Hello, world!</h1>` from the template.

We're ready to start, but we also want to write our own CSS. For that, let's create a folder called `css` and a CSS file called `styles.css`.

To do that quickly, you can right-click on the left-hand bar in Atom and click on **New Folder,** as shown in the following screenshot:

Create a folder in Atom

When you create a CSS file, you will always need to link it to your HTML file, otherwise it doesn't work. If you remember to link it, you'll have to add the following code:

```
<link rel="stylesheet" href="css/styles.css">
```

Now that we have created our CSS file and linked it to our HTML file, the last thing we need to do is to duplicate the img and fonts folders we created in our last project. This is easier, as we will recreate the same page. Just copy and paste those folders to our new project.

Don't forget to link the font CSS to your HTML. Add it before your `styles.css`:

```
<link rel="stylesheet" href="fonts/font.css">
```

Install the Google Font Roboto:

```
<link href="https://fonts.googleapis.com/css?family=Roboto:400,700"
rel="stylesheet">
```

Now that we're all set, let's get started.

Bootstrap navbar

The first thing we will create is the Bootstrap `navbar`. The `navbar` within Bootstrap is one of the most recognizable features within the Bootstrap framework due to the nature of how it works. So, to provide an example of how it works, if we navigate to the Bootstrap website and then to the **Documentation** tab, we have all the navigation elements across the top of the screen:

The Bootstrap navigation

If we shrink the browser, we can see how the navigation shrinks as well. Then, when it hits the smaller screen, we get this hamburger menu, which, if we click on it, displays the navigation elements within it:

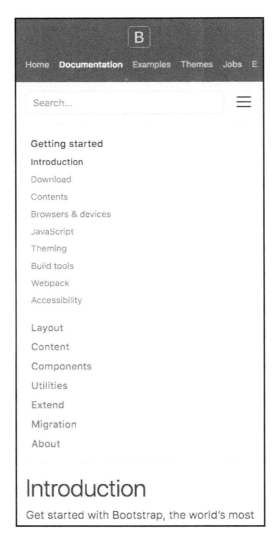

The Bootstrap mobile navigation

Coding the Bootstrap navigation

Now let's head to the `navbar` section of **Components** in our Bootstrap website. Here, you can find all the necessary documentation to build your navigation with Bootstrap.

Now let's head back to our HTML file and write the following code:

```
<nav class="navbar navbar-expand-lg fixed-top ">

</nav>
```

The details of the preceding code are as follows:

1. We start off within the body of the content by adding our `<nav>` element and all `<nav>` elements require a `navbar` class.
2. Then, we added the new expand class, which is the `navbar-expand-lg`. This essentially tells the browser when to collapse the `navbar` and when to expand it.
3. So, in this case, it will expand and show the desktop version when it hits large screens. If we wanted to expand when we hit medium screens, then we just need to change `lg` to `md` or, for smaller screens, to `sm`.
4. Then, we added the positioning class, and, because we want this `navbar` to be fixed at the top of the screen so that when the user scrolls, the navigation is always visible, we simply added the class `fixed-top`.

Next, let's add some navigation options:

```
<nav class="navbar navbar-expand-lg fixed-top ">
    <div class="collapse navbar-collapse" id="navigation-bar">
    </div>
  </nav>
```

In this code, we simply id the following things:

1. We added a `div` to the `collapse` class. This simply informs the browser that this `div` and all its content will be a collapsible element.
2. Then, we added a class of `navbar-collapse`.
3. Lastly, we added an `id="navigation-bar"` that will link to our toggle button later on.

Now we will need to add our navigation list, with a `<ul>` and `<li>` for the list and an `<a>` for every link:

```
<nav class="navbar navbar-expand-lg fixed-top ">
    <div class="collapse navbar-collapse" id="navigation-bar">
        <ul class="navbar-nav">
          <li class="nav-item"><a class="nav-link"
href="upcoming.html">Upcoming events</a></li>
          <li class="nav-item"><a class="nav-link" href="past.html">Past
events</a></li>
          <li class="nav-item"><a class="nav-link"
href="faq.html">FAQ</a></li>
          <li class="nav-item"><a class="nav-link" href="about.html">About
us</a></li>
          <li class="nav-item"><a class="nav-link"
href="blog.html">Blog</a></li>
          <li class="nav-item"><a class="nav-link"
href="contact.html">Contact</a></li>
        </ul>
      </div>
    </nav>
```

To make the navigation work properly, we will need the `.navbar-nav` class on the `<ul>` and the `nav-item` class on the `<li>`. Lastly, we will need a `.nav-link` class on the `<a>` tag.

Now let's check out our list in our browser:

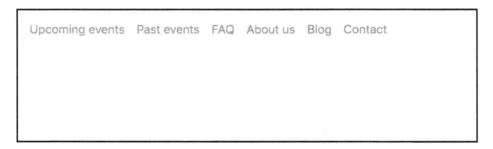

Work in progress on our navigation

We have our Bootstrap navigation, but if you shrink the page to a mobile view, you will notice that the navigation disappears. That is because we haven't included our toggle button, so let's add it now.

Back in our `index.html`, we can add our button above the `div` we created. Let's create a button tag and give it the `.navbar-toggler` class and instructions, as follows:

```
<button type="button" class="navbar-toggler" data-toggle="collapse" data-target="#navigation-bar">

</button>
```

The `data-target` attribute is how we link the navigation options that we had earlier, which is the `#navigation-bar` ID.

Now we will need to add the hamburger menu inside this button. To do that, we can use the ≡ HTML code, which is the HTML code for a three-bar icon. There are plenty of HTML symbols available that you could use. You can google HTML symbols and that will provide you with plenty of examples and symbols.

Let's add a `span` tag with the `.navbar-toggler-icon` class and the HTML symbol inside:

```
<button type="button" class="navbar-toggler" data-toggle="collapse" data-target="#navigation-bar">
    <span class="navbar-toggler-icon">≡</span>
</button>
```

Now, if we save and check it, we can see our menu icon on a mobile screen, and if we click on it, the menu appears correctly:

Mobile navigation.

Now let's add the logo in our `navbar`. Usually, the logo is a link, so let's add a `<a>` tag with the `.navbar-brand` class.

We don't want the logo to collapse on mobile view, so we'll just add `<a>` before the `<button>`:

```
<nav class="navbar navbar-expand-lg fixed-top ">

    <a class="navbar-brand" href="#"><img src="img/logo.png" class="img-
fluid" alt="Logo Racing Club"></a>
        <button type="button" class="navbar-toggler" data-toggle="collapse"
data-target="#navigation-bar">
            <span class="navbar-toggler-icon">≡</span>
        </button>

        <div class="collapse navbar-collapse" id="navigation-bar">
            <ul class="navbar-nav">
                <li class="nav-item"><a class="nav-link"
href="upcoming.html">Upcoming events</a></li>
                <li class="nav-item"><a class="nav-link" href="past.html">Past
events</a></li>
                <li class="nav-item"><a class="nav-link"
href="faq.html">FAQ</a></li>
                <li class="nav-item"><a class="nav-link" href="about.html">About
us</a></li>
                <li class="nav-item"><a class="nav-link"
href="blog.html">Blog</a></li>
                <li class="nav-item"><a class="nav-link"
href="contact.html">Contact</a></li>
            </ul>
        </div>
    </nav>
```

In this `<a>`, we added the following:

1. A class `.navbar-brand`
2. An `img` tag linked with our logo
3. In this `img`, we added a `.img-fluid` class that makes this image responsive

We have our logo set now, but it's not done yet. We will need to add the right-hand side navigation. To do that, we simply need to add another `<ul>` after our `<ul class="navbar-nav">`:

```
<div class="collapse navbar-collapse" id="navigation-bar">
        <ul class="navbar-nav">
            <li class="nav-item"><a class="nav-link"
href="upcoming.html">Upcoming events</a></li>
            <li class="nav-item"><a class="nav-link" href="past.html">Past
events</a></li>
```

```
            <li class="nav-item"><a class="nav-link"
href="faq.html">FAQ</a></li>
            <li class="nav-item"><a class="nav-link" href="about.html">About
us</a></li>
            <li class="nav-item"><a class="nav-link"
href="blog.html">Blog</a></li>
            <li class="nav-item"><a class="nav-link"
href="contact.html">Contact</a></li>
        </ul>

        <ul class="navbar-nav ml-auto">
            <li class="nav-item"><a class="nav-link"
href="login.html">Login</a></li>
            <li class="nav-item"><span class="nav-link"><iframe
src="https://www.facebook.com/plugins/like.php?href=http%3A%2F%2Ffacebook.c
om%2Fphilippehongcreative&width=51&layout=button&action=like&size=small&sho
w_faces=false&share=false&height=65&appId=235448876515718" width="51"
height="20" style="border:none;overflow:hidden"></iframe></span></li>
        </ul>
    </div>
```

We added the `.ml-auto` class to move this second navigation to the right. This stands for `margin-left` automatic. It fills the margin on the left-hand side of our navigation, which will effectively shift it to the right-hand side. If you wanted the opposite effect, you would simply add the `.mr-auto` class.

Now let's take a look at our navigation:

Bootstrap navigation

Our navigation looks awesome, and we have all the elements that we need for the navigation bar. Next, we will add some styles.

Styling our navigation bar

Styling Bootstrap components is fairly simple. The only thing we need to do is to overwrite the Bootstrap CSS. However, we don't want to overwrite Bootstrap CSS files themselves; the only thing we want to do is add additional CSS properties that will overwrite the original Bootstrap CSS. We have beforehand created a CSS file called `styles.css`, and, since this file is linked after the Bootstrap CSS file in order on the HTML document, every CSS we write having the same properties and class will overwrite the original Bootstrap CSS:

```
<link rel="stylesheet"
href="https://maxcdn.bootstrapcdn.com/bootstrap/4.0.0/css/bootstrap.min.css
" integrity="sha384-
Gn5384xqQ1aoWXA+058RXPxPg6fy4IWvTNh0E263XmFcJlSAwiGgFAW/dAiS6JXm"
crossorigin="anonymous">
<link rel="stylesheet" href="css/styles.css">
```

We need to target the right CSS class to overwrite it. If you remember, we used Google Chrome's **Inspector** to inspect elements and check their CSS. To open the **Inspector** (or **Developer Tool**), right-click on the element and click on **Inspect:**

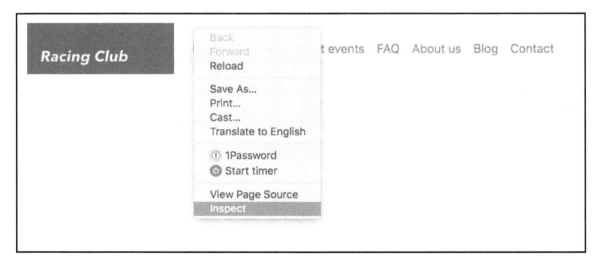

The Inspect element on Chrome

Now we can see the developer panel, and there is a lot of information there. You can check the different panels available. When hovering over an element in the HTML, you can see it displayed on the web page itself:

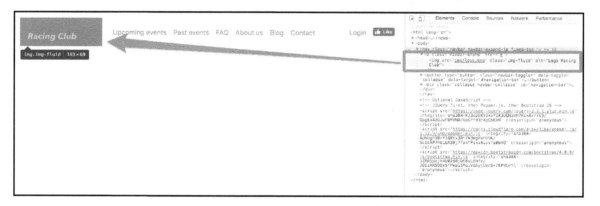

The Google Chrome Inspector

This is very useful when you want to fix any CSS style issues or look at the HTML. Let's fix the CSS now.

With the **Inspector**, we can see that the `.navbar` class has some padding by default, but we want to get rid of it.

Simply add the following CSS to your `styles.css`:

```
.navbar {
  padding: 0;
}
```

After saving, you can check that we overwrote the bootstrap CSS with our own:

Overwriting the Bootstrap CSS

Now that you understand the principle, we can quickly fix the navigation:

```
.navbar {
  padding: 0;
  background-image: linear-gradient(0deg, rgba(0,0,0,0.00) 0%,
rgba(0,0,0,0.50) 50%);
}

.navbar-brand {
  padding: 0;
}

.navbar-nav li a {
  color: white;
  text-decoration: none;
  font-family: 'built_titling', Helvetica, sans-serif;
  font-weight: 200;
  font-size: 20px;
  letter-spacing: 4px;
}

.navbar-collapse {
  padding: 10px 15px;
}

@media (min-width: 992px) {
  .navbar-collapse {
    padding: 0;
  }
}

.navbar-toggler-icon {
  color: white;
}
```

The preceding code will stylize the navbar correctly. You can see that everything is functional without too many lines of code, even the responsive part. That's the power of Bootstrap. If we compare what we've done to make the navigation responsive, with jQuery and all the media queries, we've written a lot less code than we did for the first project. Let's move on to the hero section now.

Styling the hero section

Now that we understand how to use Bootstrap, we can start to use other components in Bootstrap's library:

```
<!-- HERO SECTION -->

    <div class="hero position-relative overflow-hidden d-flex align-items-
center">
      <div class="container">
        <div class="col-md-7 my-auto">
          <p class="lead font-weight-normal">13.05.17</p>
          <h1 class="display-2 font-weight-normal custom-font-
title">WAKEFIELD PARK</h1>
          <a class="btn btn-primary" href="#">Book now</a>
        </div>
      </div>
    </div>

<!-- END HERO SECTION -->
```

Let me explain the preceding piece of code a bit.

For the *first* `div` it is as follows:

1. We first set a custom class—`.hero`—so that we can apply a custom code in the parent element.
2. We add the utility classes `.position-relative` and `.overflow-hidden` provided by Bootstrap so we don't have to apply them in the CSS.
3. The class `.d-flex` will set the display on `display: flex`.
4. The utility class `.align-items-center` will align the child elements so that they are vertically centered.
5. We add a custom font `.custom-font-title` so that we can add to every element with a custom font.

We then apply a *second* `div` with the `.container` class so that we can apply the Bootstrap default `container` class.

The following classes are all part of the Bootstrap library. You can see them on the Bootstrap website.

The next part is to customize the `.hero` class we added:

```css
.hero {
  width: 100%;
  height: 700px;
  background-image:
    linear-gradient(to bottom, rgba(0,0,0,0.3) 0%,rgba(0,0,0,0.4) 100%),
    url("../img/hero-image.jpg");
  background-repeat: no-repeat;
  background-size: cover;
  background-position: center;
  color: white;
}
```

Save, and take a look at what we have:

Preview of the hero section

Now let's add the final touch to it:

```css
.custom-font-title {
  font-family: 'built_titling', Helvetica, sans-serif;
  font-weight: 400;
}

.btn-primary {
  font-size: 18px;
  letter-spacing: 4.5px;
  background: #BF0000;
  color: white;
  font-family: 'built_titling', Helvetica, sans-serif;
  font-weight: 400;
  padding: 12px 22px;
  border: none;
  outline: none;
  transition: all 0.3s ease;
  border-radius: 0px;
}

.btn-primary:hover {
  background: #A3171B;
}

.btn-primary:active {
  box-shadow: inset 0px 8px 4px rgba(0, 0, 0, 0.25);
  background: #A3171B!important;
  box-shadow: none!important;

}

.btn-primary:focus {
  box-shadow: inset 0px 8px 4px rgba(0, 0, 0, 0.25);
  background: #A3171B;
  box-shadow: none;
}
```

This will overwrite the default style of Bootstrap for the heading and primary button:

Our final hero section

Let's start the **Blog** section now.

Styling the Blog section

With the earlier website that we built, we had our own grid system. However, now, we can simply use Bootstrap grid, which is way better and more practical than the one we created.

Let's start with the HTML:

```
<div class="blog py-5">
    <div class="container">
      <div class="row">
        <div class="col-md-4">
          <div class="card mb-4">
            <img class="card-img-top" alt="Thumbnail Blog" src="img/blog-
img/blog1.jpg">
            <div class="card-body">
              <small class="text-muted">09th January 2016</small>
```

```
            <h4 class="font-weight-bold">Racing Club Advan Neova
Challenge Round 3 Update</h4>
            <p class="card-text">FINAL ROUND: Labour Day Trackday
Wakefield Park. Last chance to compete in the Circuit Club Advan Neova
Challenge 2016!
There was much anticipation with Jason's big power Evo competing at Round
3, however some suspected engi... </p>
            <a href="#" class="btn btn-outline-primary">Read more</a>
         </div>
      </div>
    </div>
  </div>
</div>
```

In the preceding code, you can note that there are a lot of `.py-5` `.my-5` classes. Those classes are spacing classes; they've been added to the last version of Bootstrap, so you can add spacing just with a simple class. To understand how you can use them, navigate to the **Spacing** section in the **Utilities** section of the documentation:

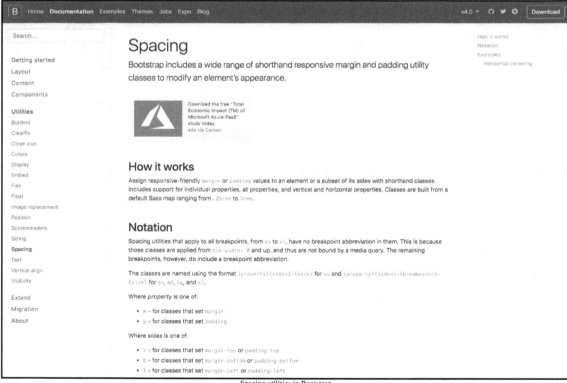

Spacing utilities in Bootstrap

Also, you would have noticed we used the grid for each card. The grid is a bit tricky to understand at first, but, once you get it, it's very powerful and useful. The best thing to do is to play around with it. You can play around with the grid by checking the given examples at https://getbootstrap.com/docs/4.0/layout/grid/.

Here, we added the .col-md-4 class because we want three same blocks with the same width, as Bootstrap works with a 12-column system—12 divided by 3 equals 4. Furthermore, we used the md property so that it only applies when the browser resolution is bigger than 768px.

Let's now duplicate the card six times for our six blog posts:

```
<!-- BLOG SECTION -->

    <div class="blog py-5">
      <div class="container">
        <div class="row">
          <div class="col-md-4">
            <div class="card mb-4">
              <img class="card-img-top" alt="Thumbnail Blog" src="img/blog-
img/blog1.jpg">
              <div class="card-body">
                <small class="text-muted">09th January 2016</small>
                <h4 class="font-weight-bold">Racing Club Advan Neova
Challenge Round 3 Update</h4>
                <p class="card-text">FINAL ROUND: Labour Day Trackday
Wakefield Park. Last chance to compete in the Circuit Club Advan Neova
Challenge 2016!
There was much anticipation with Jason's big power Evo competing at Round
3, however some suspected engi... </p>
                <a href="#" class="btn btn-outline-primary">Read more</a>
              </div>
            </div>
          </div>
          <div class="col-md-4">
            <div class="card mb-4">
              <img class="card-img-top" alt="Thumbnail Blog" src="img/blog-
img/blog2.jpg">
              <div class="card-body">
                <small class="text-muted">09th January 2016</small>
                <h4 class="font-weight-bold">Hidden Behind the Scenes</h4>
                <p class="card-text">Originally posted by Narada Kudinar,
23.08.11.
At our Trackdays, we get a variety - owners with their girlfriends, owners
with their mates, owners and their mechanics - but there is one combination
I am truly at envy with. It's the owners and their Dads. </p>
```

```
              <a href="#" class="btn btn-outline-primary">Read more</a>
            </div>
          </div>
        </div>
        <div class="col-md-4">
          <div class="card mb-4">
            <img class="card-img-top" alt="Thumbnail Blog" src="img/blog-
img/blog3.jpg">
            <div class="card-body">
              <small class="text-muted">04th July 2013</small>
              <h4 class="font-weight-bold">Introducing Advan
Trackdays!</h4>
              <p class="card-text">For the first time, Yokohama Advan
Tyres are hosting their very own Trackdays, hosted by your's truly! The
aim? To thank their loyal customers by providing a bargain event as well as
introduce new Advan tyres to those who don't use them yet.. </p>
              <a href="#" class="btn btn-outline-primary">Read more</a>
            </div>
          </div>
        </div>
        <div class="col-md-4">
          <div class="card mb-4">
            <img class="card-img-top" alt="Thumbnail Blog" src="img/blog-
img/blog4.jpg">
            <div class="card-body">
              <small class="text-muted">03th January 2016</small>
              <h4 class="font-weight-bold">ANZAC Day Spots Running
Out!</h4>
              <p class="card-text">FINAL ROUND: Labour Day Trackday
Wakefield Park. Last chance to compete in the Circuit Club Advan Neova
Challenge 2016!
There was much anticipation with Jason's big power Evo competing at Round
3, however some suspected engi... </p>
              <a href="#" class="btn btn-outline-primary">Read more</a>
            </div>
          </div>
        </div>
        <div class="col-md-4">
          <div class="card mb-4">
            <img class="card-img-top" alt="Thumbnail Blog" src="img/blog-
img/blog5.jpg">
            <div class="card-body">
              <small class="text-muted">02th January 2016</small>
              <h4 class="font-weight-bold">10 Year Anniversary Details
Now Available!</h4>
              <p class="card-text">Originally posted by Narada Kudinar,
23.08.11.
At our Trackdays, we get a variety - owners with their girlfriends, owners
```

```
with their mates, owners and their mechanics - but there is one combination
I am truly at envy with. It's the owners and their Dads.</p>
                <a href="#" class="btn btn-outline-primary">Read more</a>
            </div>
          </div>
        </div>
        <div class="col-md-4">
          <div class="card mb-4">
            <img class="card-img-top" alt="Thumbnail Blog" src="img/blog-
img/blog6.jpg">
            <div class="card-body">
              <small class="text-muted">01th January 2016</small>
              <h4 class="font-weight-bold">Prepare for EPICNESS</h4>
              <p class="card-text">For the first time, Yokohama Advan
Tyres are hosting their very own Trackdays, hosted by your's truly! The
aim? To thank their loyal customers by providing a bargain event as well as
introduce new Advan tyres to those who don't use them yet... </p>
                <a href="#" class="btn btn-outline-primary">Read more</a>
            </div>
          </div>
        </div>
      </div>
    </div>

    <!-- END BLOG SECTION -->
```

The last thing is to add the **Show more** button. We also need to center the button
horizontally. For that, we'll use the `.d-flex` flexbox Bootstrap class paired with
the `.align-items-center` class:

```
<div class="row d-flex align-items-center py-5">
    <div class="mx-auto">
        <a href="#" class="btn btn-primary">Show more</a>
    </div>
</div>
```

Finally, to make it centered, we just need to add the `.mx-auto` class, so the left and right
margins are in auto.

Let's check what we have now:

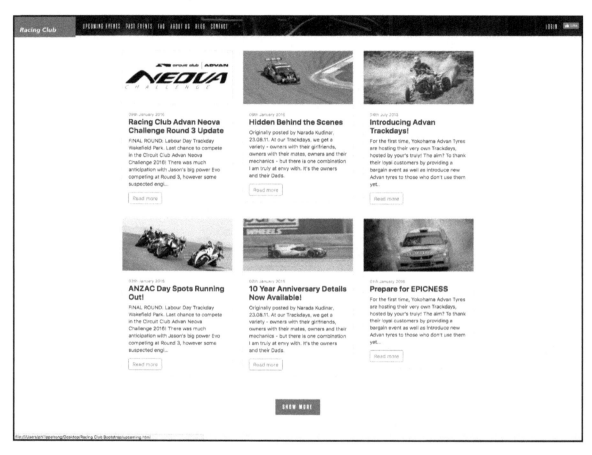

Work in progress – the Blog section

We have something pretty neat, without any styling at all. The only thing left is to customize the cards and the outline button, and we're good to go:

```css
body {
    font-family: 'Roboto', sans-serif;
}

.btn-outline-primary {
  color: #BF0000;
  background-color: transparent;
  background-image: none;
  border-color: #BF0000;
}

.btn-outline-primary:hover {
  background: #A3171B;
  border-color: #A3171B;
}

.btn-outline-primary:active {
  box-shadow: inset 0px 8px 4px rgba(0, 0, 0, 0.25);
  background: #A3171B!important;
  box-shadow: none!important;
  outline: none;
  border-color: #A3171B!important;

}

.btn-outline-primary:focus {
  box-shadow: inset 0px 8px 4px rgba(0, 0, 0, 0.25);
  background: #A3171B;
  box-shadow: none;
  outline: none;
}

.card {
  border: none;
}
```

The following is the final stage of the design:

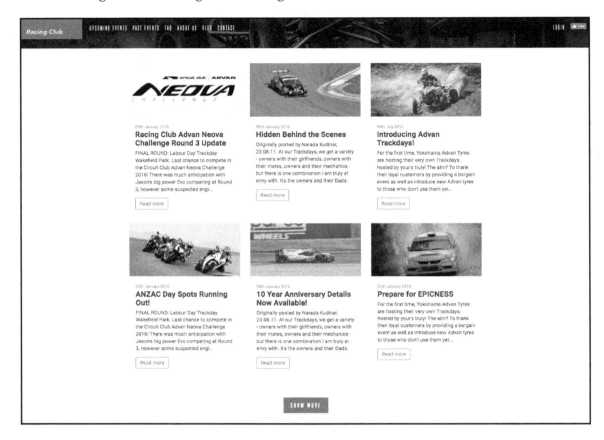

The design finalized in the blog section

That's it; we're all done with the **Blog** section. Let's start the **ABOUT US** section.

Styling the about section

This section is pretty straightforward. We'll reuse the same class as previously used. You can observe the following HTML code:

```html
<!-- ABOUT SECTION -->

    <div class="about position-relative py-5">
      <div class="container">
        <div class="row d-flex align-items-center py-5">
          <div class="col-md-6 my-auto">
            <h1 class="display-1 font-weight-normal custom-font-title text-
white">The<br /> Love<br /> of car</h1>
          </div>
          <div class="col-md-6 my-auto">
            <h3 class="font-weight-normal custom-font-title text-
white">About us</h3>
            <p class="lead font-weight-normal text-white">Circuit Club was
founded in 2003 with one goal in mind, to make motorsport accessible
through Trackdays. What started out simply as a bunch of mates with a love
of cars and driving fast...</p>
            <a class="btn btn-primary" href="#">Learn more</a>
          </div>
        </div>
      </div>
    </div>

<!-- END ABOUT SECTION -->
```

The only new class we used is the `.text-white` class. It's a utility class of Bootstrap that lets you color the font with some primary colors. You can access the document at `https://getbootstrap.com/docs/4.0/utilities/colors/`:

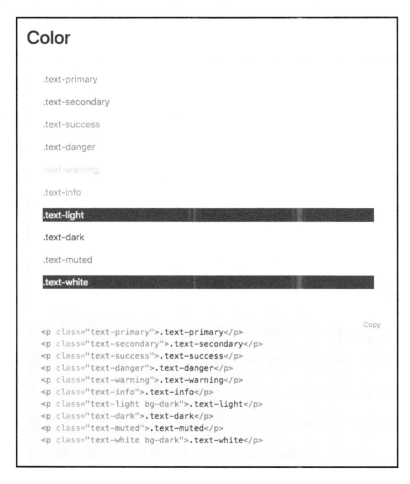

Color

.text-primary

.text-secondary

.text-success

.text-danger

.text-warning

.text-info

.text-light

.text-dark

.text-muted

.text-white

Copy

```
<p class="text-primary">.text-primary</p>
<p class="text-secondary">.text-secondary</p>
<p class="text-success">.text-success</p>
<p class="text-danger">.text-danger</p>
<p class="text-warning">.text-warning</p>
<p class="text-info">.text-info</p>
<p class="text-light bg-dark">.text-light</p>
<p class="text-dark">.text-dark</p>
<p class="text-muted">.text-muted</p>
<p class="text-white bg-dark">.text-white</p>
```

Text color classes in Bootstrap.

For the CSS, we only need to add the background and a little styling on the title:

```
.about {
  background-image: url(../img/about-us-bg.jpg);
  background-repeat: no-repeat;
  background-size: cover;
}
```

```
.about h1.display-1::after {
  content: "";
  display: block;
  background: #BF0000;
  width: 90px;
  height: 2px;
  margin-top: 30px;
}
```

Let's take a look at how it looks:

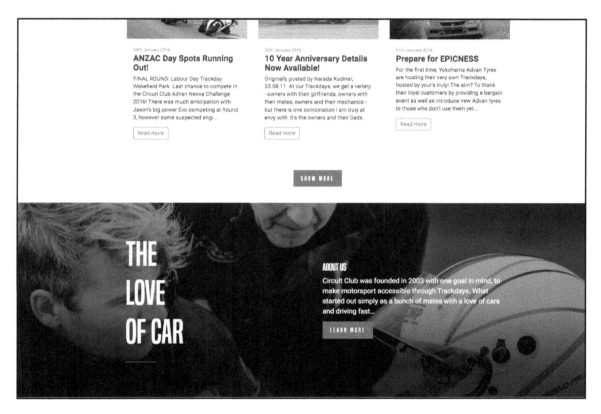

The About Us section

This **About Us** section was pretty easy; let's continue to the **PARTNERS** section.

Styling the partner section

For the **PARTNERS** section, we set the HTML to something such as this:

```html
<!-- PARTNERS SECTION -->

    <div class="partners position-relative py-5">
      <div class="container py-5">
        <h3 class="display-3 custom-font-title text-white text-
center">PARTNERS</h3>
        <div class="row d-flex justify-content-center py-5">
          <div class="my-auto text-center px-3">
            <img class="pb-2" src="img/partner1.png" alt="Partners Racing
Club">
            <p class="font-weight-normal text-white">Advan Neova Cup</p>
          </div>
          <div class="my-auto text-center px-3">
            <img class="pb-2" src="img/partner2.png" alt="Partners Racing
Club">
            <p class="font-weight-normal text-white">JDM Style Tuning</p>
          </div>
        </div>
        <div class="row d-flex align-items-center pb-5">
          <div class="mx-auto">
            <a href="#" class="btn btn-primary">Show more</a>
          </div>
        </div>
      </div>
    </div>

<!-- END PARTNERS SECTION -->
```

In the preceding code, we used the class `.justify-content-center` to horizontally center the two partners. Everything else is pretty simple.

In terms of CSS, the only thing we had to do was change the color of the background to black:

```css
.partners {
  background: #000;
}
```

It's done! How easy was it?:

The PARTNERS section

Let's head to the final step, that is, the footer.

Styling the footer

For the footer, things will get a bit more complex. The HTML will be something like this:

```
<!-- FOOTER -->
    <nav class="footer">
      <div class="container d-md-flex align-items-center py-md-5">
        <a class="navbar-brand" href="#"><img src="img/logo-footer.png"
```

```
class="img-fluid pl-3" alt="Logo Racing Club"></a>
        <ul class="nav d-block d-md-flex pt-5 pt-md-0">
        <li class="nav-item"><a class="nav-link text-white"
href="upcoming.html">Upcoming events</a></li>
        <li class="nav-item"><a class="nav-link text-white"
href="past.html">Past events</a></li>
        <li class="nav-item"><a class="nav-link text-white"
href="faq.html">FAQ</a></li>
        <li class="nav-item"><a class="nav-link text-white"
href="about.html">About us</a></li>
        <li class="nav-item"><a class="nav-link text-white"
href="blog.html">Blog</a></li>
        <li class="nav-item"><a class="nav-link text-white"
href="contact.html">Contact</a></li>
        </ul>

        <ul class="nav ml-auto d-block d-md-flex pb-5 pb-md-0">
        <li class="nav-item"><a class="nav-link text-white"
href="login.html">Login</a></li>
        <li class="nav-item"><span class="nav-link"><iframe
src="https://www.facebook.com/plugins/like.php?href=http%3A%2F%2Ffacebook.c
om%2Fphilippehongcreative&width=51&layout=button&action=like&size=small&sho
w_faces=false&share=false&height=65&appId=235448876515718" width="51"
height="20" style="border:none;overflow:hidden"></iframe></span></li>
        </ul>
    </div>
    </nav>
    <!-- END FOOTER -->
```

In a lot of Bootstrap classes, there are some responsive utility classes you can apply, and they're always with the same references: xs, sm, md, and lg. For example, for the .d-flex class, you can apply the responsive utility class when you need to. By adding .d-md-flex, you apply the display:flex property only on medium screens. This is very useful and can be applied to a lot of Bootstrap classes.

With the good use of classes, the only CSS we needed to write was the following:

```
.footer {
  background: #000;
}

.footer .nav-link {
  text-decoration: none;
  font-family: 'built_titling', Helvetica, sans-serif;
  font-weight: 200;
  font-size: 20px;
  letter-spacing: 4px;
}
```

This is what our footer looks like:

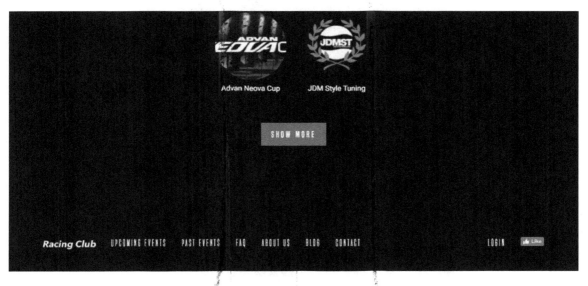

Our footer section

It's fully responsive:

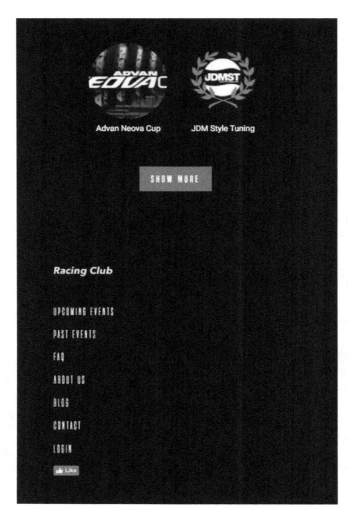

The footer section on mobile

Summary

You saw how Bootstrap can help you in your development phase. If you can master the use of Bootstrap, you can really kick-start or implement any project with ease and efficiency. This is why so many developers love Bootstrap, and you should too.

What's next? Next, we will have an introduction to server-side rendering and why it's the new development trend. Let's go.

13
Introduction to Client-Side Rendering

Since the beginning of the web, as we have learned, the conventional method of displaying HTML is using **server-side rendering**. This latter was great; websites were simple and didn't need much interaction. However, nowadays, that's not the case anymore. There are a lot of applications on a single website; you need messaging, updates, shopping, real-time data sync—the end consumer always wants more.

In this chapter, you'll learn the following things:

- What is a server-side rendering?
- What is a client-side rendering?
- The pros and cons of both
- An introduction to VueJS
- Finally, creating a Weather application with VueJS

So, what is this **client-side rendering**? Client-side rendering is a new type of rendering website using mostly JavaScript to render it instead of server-side languages such as PHP, Python, or Ruby.

To understand the difference, we will need to understand how server-side rendering works.

What is server-side rendering?

Server-side rendering is the most common way to render a website. Whenever you visit a website, a request to the server is made, and it renders the website in HTML. This usually takes a few milliseconds, but it will depend on many factors, such as internet speed, location, and the number of visitors.

If you want to visit another website, you basically perform another request to the server with the same process all over again. This can be annoying if your page has a thousand lines of code, like many of the websites do nowadays.

However, server-side rendering is good for SEO, as the HTML page is there for robots to crawl, something that client-side rendering doesn't do well, at least not as simple as server-side rendering.

What is client-side rendering?

Client-side rendering, on the other, is rendered with JavaScript. Instead of getting the HTML by itself, you're getting a simple HTML structure but with JavaScript to render the rest of the HTML with your browser.

This is a new approach and has gained a lot of traction lately with the development of framework from companies such as Facebook and Google.

The main difference is that when you click to take a look at another page, the JavaScript renders the page instead of requesting a new page from the server. This is a much faster way to load content, as it will only load content that it needs instead of the whole page.

The downside of it is that it's very bad SEO-wise, since the content is not rendered until the page is loaded into the browser. This can be fixed, but not in an easy way yet.

Pros and cons of server and client-side rendering

The next two sections are a quick a summary of the pros and cons of each, so you can decide which you'll use for each project.

Server-side rendering

Pros:

- Better SEO because search engines can crawl the site
- The initial page loads faster
- Good for static sites

Cons:

- Frequent server requests
- Slower rendering
- Page has to reload every time

Client-side rendering

Pros:

- Faster rendering after the initial load
- Good for web applications
- Fewer requests to the server

Cons:

- Bad SEO if not implemented correctly
- The initial load may require more time
- Requires an external library in most cases

Introducing to VueJS

They are many JavaScript frameworks we can use if we want to build a client-side rendering website. ReactJS, AngularJS, and VueJS are among the most well-known frameworks—not surprising when you know that they're backed by Google and Facebook.

VueJS is one of the easiest to learn. That's why we chose to start with this one. In the last chapter of this book, we'll do a quick introduction to VueJS so that you can understand how it works and what are the possibilities for it:

VueJS homepage

VueJS allows you to create everything from small widgets, driven by JavaScript, which you drop into existing applications. Over medium-sized applications where you control the whole page through JavaScript and therefore re-render various parts, making it very reactive, and all the way up to building big enterprise-level applications, single-page application, where your whole web page, multiple pages (at least it feels like this to the user), are driven by VueJS, which renders significant parts of the DOMs, to make it look like they were different pages being loaded, but, in the end, JavaScript handles all of that.

Why JavaScript? Since JavaScript runs in the browser, you don't need to reach out to any server and wait for any responses if you only want to re-render parts of the application. This makes the application very reactive, makes it feel nice, and provides awesome user experiences.

This is what you can do with VueJS. Now, why would you choose VueJS and not, let's say, Angular 2 or ReactJS, which you may know and does a similar thing. Well, first of all, VueJS is extremely lean and small regarding the file size. We're talking about 16 kilobytes, minified in gzip, for the core framework.

It's a very focused and to-the-point framework. However, it's not only small, hence providing a fast loading time, it's also fast at runtime, and, judging by some benchmarks, it even beats Angular 2 and ReactJS. Now, of course, it will always depend on your specific application.

I'd say let's dive right into it now and get started with VueJS and build our first little application and take a look at how we can actually get it set up.

Setting up VueJS

Getting started with VueJS and creating your first application is actually very simple. We start on vuejs.org, its official home page; there, you will note this nice **Get Started** button. Let's click on it. It takes you to the official documentation, which is always worth taking a look at anyway, but, there, we want to go to installation. Now, here, you've got a couple of different options, depending on which kind of setup you want to use:

The VueJS Installation page

There are different options to download VueJS—we can either download the file or use the CDN provided. For this exercise, we'll simply use the CDN. Simply click on the link provided by VueJS, as follows:

```
# CDN

We recommend linking to a specific version number that you can update manually:

  <script src="https://cdn.jsdelivr.net/npm/vue@2.5.16/dist/vue.js"></script>

You can browse the source of the NPM package at cdn.jsdelivr.net/npm/vue.

Vue is also available on unpkg and cdnjs (cdnjs takes some time to sync so the latest release
may not be available yet).

Make sure to read about the different builds of Vue and use the production
version in your published site, replacing  vue.js  with  vue.min.js . This is a smaller build
optimized for speed instead of development experience.
```

VueJS CDN

Now, instead of creating a new HTML project, let's go to `jsfiddle.net`.

JSFiddle is an online web editor, so you can simply create or test something very easily:

JSFiddle

Simply copy and paste the script from VueJS to the HTML `block` section:

```
<script src="https://cdn.jsdelivr.net/npm/vue@2.5.16/dist/VueJS"></script>
```

You can remove the `@2.5.16` and leave just the `vue` so that it will always fetch the latest version:

```
<script src="https://cdn.jsdelivr.net/npm/vue/dist/VueJS"></script>
```

Now that we've imported VueJS, we can already use it with all its features. So, let's use it and build our first little application. For that, I want to add a paragraph, in which I want to say `Hello world`:

```
<p>
Hello world!
</p>
```

So far, there has been nothing interesting. However, what we want to do is to be able to control the text with VueJS. To do that, we will need to create an instance. In VueJS, you will simply need to add the following code in our JavaScript file:

```
var app = new Vue({
})
```

Now, I will need to create a `div` that will contain my app, as we don't want our `<p>` tag to be the app. We'll add an ID app:

```
<div id="app">
    <p>
        Hello world!
    </p>
</div>
```

Now we will need to call the `#app div` and set it as our template for our app:

```
var app = new Vue({
    el: '#app',
})
```

Now, to put any data into our app, we will need the `data` property:

```
var app = new Vue({
    el: '#app',
    data: {
      title: "Hello World!"
    }
})
```

We can call it `title`. Now we will need to link it to our text; to do that, just remove the text and add `{{ title }}` or the name of the property.

Let's run this with JSFiddle by clicking on the **RUN** button on the top-left corner:

```
HTML ▼                                                           CSS ▼

    <script src="https://cdn.jsdelivr.net/npm/vue/dist/vue.js"></script>

    <div id="app">
        <p>
            {{title}}
        </p>
    </div>



JavaScript + No-Library (pure JS) ▼                              Hello World!

        var app = new Vue({
           el: '#app',
           data: {
            title: "Hello World!"
            }
        })
```

The first VueJS instance

Now, you're probably going to say that there is no point in doing that. It's not done yet. Let's extend our VueJS application by adding an input that will be linked to the text displayed in the `<p>`:

```
<input v-model="title" type="text">
```

We added a `v-model` directive to the input; this will bind the textbox to the data property `title` in Vue.

You can try now by adding any text; it will follow what you write:

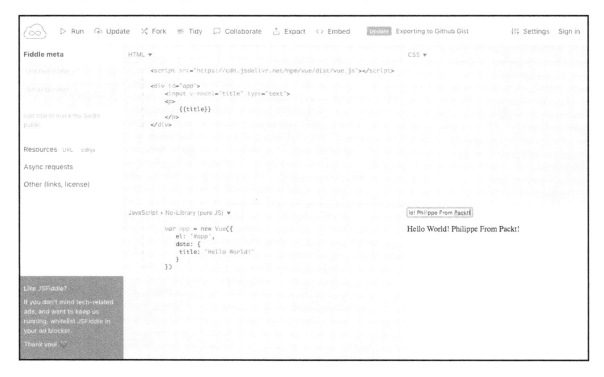

The JSFiddle end of the exercise

This introduction is now finished. You can access my JSfiddle if you have any trouble with this step at `https://jsfiddle.net/knee8oha/9/`.

For me, the best way to learn is by practicing. So, let's create an app together for you to be familiar with VueJS.

Creating a weather application in VueJS

In this exercise, we will build a component that we can use to display the weather of a location in VueJS. This component will be created with a location search textbox; this will then search for `http://openweathermap.org/`, which is a free weather API, so we can get the information for the location-based search.

Vue Material

Let's create a simple HTML file. For this exercise, we'll not use Bootstrap but, instead, use another library and take a look at how easy it is. We'll use Vue Material, which is a library based on Google Material design. You can check it out at `https://vuematerial.io/`:

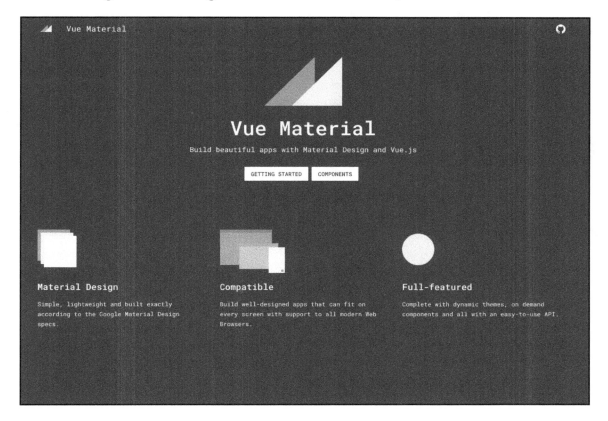

Vue Material

Let's head to their installation instruction by clicking on **Getting started**. Fortunately, they provide a CDN with a template ready to use. Let's copy their template and paste it into our HTML file:

```
<!doctype html>
<html>
  <head>
    <meta charset="utf-8">
    <meta content="width=device-width,initial-scale=1,minimal-ui"
name="viewport">
```

```
    <link rel="stylesheet"
href="https://fonts.googleapis.com/css?family=Roboto:300,400,500,700,400ita
lic|Material+Icons">
    <link rel="stylesheet"
href="https://unpkg.com/vue-material@beta/dist/vue-material.min.css">
    <link rel="stylesheet"
href="https://unpkg.com/vue-material@beta/dist/theme/default.css">
  </head>

  <body>
    <div id="app">
      <!-- Your code here -->
    </div>

    <script src="https://unpkg.com/vue"></script>
    <script src="https://unpkg.com/vue-material@beta"></script>
    <script>
      Vue.use(VueMaterial.default)

      new Vue({
        el: '#app'
      })
    </script>
  </body>
</html>
```

Let's first add a title to our `<head>` section:

```
<title>Vue JS Weather App</title>
```

Vue Material provides handy layouts that we can reuse. We want the app to be mobile first with a header. We can use the following code that we insert into our app:

```
<div id="app">
    <div class="page-container">
      <md-app md-waterfall md-mode="fixed-last">
        <md-app-toolbar class="md-primary">
          <div class="md-toolbar-row">
            <div class="md-toolbar-section-start">
              <span class="md-title">VueJS: Weather</span>
            </div>

            <div class="md-toolbar-section-end">
              <md-button class="md-icon-button">
                <md-icon>more_vert</md-icon>
              </md-button>
            </div>
          </div>
```

```
      </md-app-toolbar>

      <md-app-content>
        <!-- OUR APP HERE -->
      </md-app-content>
    </md-app>
  </div>
</div>
```

Now, in our `<script>` section, we will want to mount the app:

```
<script>

    Vue.use(VueMaterial.default)
    var weather = {
      el: '#app'
    }
    var app = new Vue(weather)
    app.$mount("#app")

</script>
```

We have now an app ready to use and totally responsive:

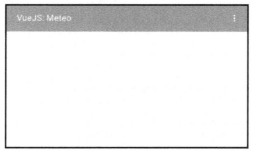

Our VueJS app

Components

The first component we will create is the main weather component. We need the following three properties attached to it:

- Data
- Methods
- Template

The data array will need the data points of the following components:

- `weatherLocation`: This will store the location entered in the input
- `weatherApi`: This is your open weather API key `http://openweathermap.org/appid`
- `weather`: We will store the results of the API in this component
- `displayWeather`: We will set a value of true or false (Boolean) if we want to display the data

To make a call to the OpenWeather API, we will use Vue resource method for `.get()`. The results of this method will be stored in the weather data point and then set the `displayWeather` data point to `true`.

OpenWeather API

To be able to access the API, we will need to sign up and create an account. Without further ado, let's create an account at `http://openweathermap.org/appid`:

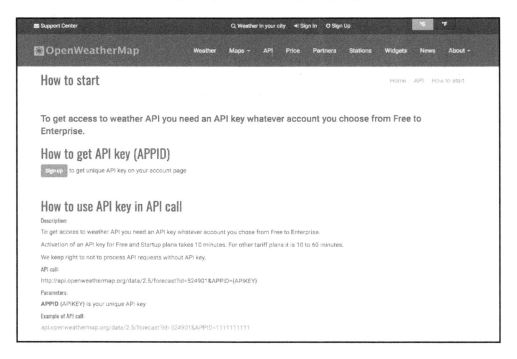

The OpenWeather signup page

Click on **Sign Up** and follow the process. In the end, you'll access a member dashboard with the API tab. You can copy the API key provided:

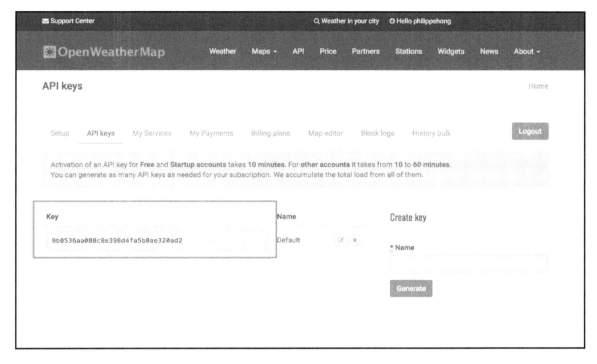

The OpenWeather API

Now let's check out how to call the API and get results. If we go on to the documentation provided by OpenWeather (`http://openweathermap.org/current`), you can get an example of an API call:

By city name

Description:

You can call by city name or city name and country code. API responds with a list of results that match a searching word.

> There is a possibility to receive a central district of the city/town with its own parameters (geographic coordinates/id/name) in API response. Example

API call:

api.openweathermap.org/data/2.5/weather?q={city name}

api.openweathermap.org/data/2.5/weather?q={city name},{country code}

Parameters:

q city name and country code divided by comma, use ISO 3166 country codes

Examples of API calls:

api.openweathermap.org/data/2.5/weather?q=London

api.openweathermap.org/data/2.5/weather?q=London,uk

API Documentation

The URL is composed like this:

ⓘ **samples.openweathermap.org**/data/2.5/weather?q=London,uk&appid=b6907d289e10d714a6e88b30761fae22

Location   API Key

API Call URL

The result we get from this call looks like this (you can test yourself):

```
{"coord":{"lon":-0.13,"lat":51.51},"weather":[{"id":300,"main":"Drizzle","d
escription":"light intensity
drizzle","icon":"09d"}],"base":"stations","main":{"temp":280.32,"pressure":
1012,"humidity":81,"temp_min":279.15,"temp_max":281.15},"visibility":10000,
"wind":{"speed":4.1,"deg":80},"clouds":{"all":90},"dt":1485789600,"sys":{"t
ype":1,"id":5091,"message":0.0103,"country":"GB","sunrise":1485762037,"suns
et":1485794875},"id":2643743,"name":"London","cod":200}
```

The code provided is in JSON, a format used generally when displaying data. The code is minified, so it is harder to read. Let's use a tool to un-minify it. I used `http://unminify. com/`. To do that, just paste the code and click on **Unminify**:

```
{
    "coord": {
        "lon": -0.13, "lat": 51.51
    }
    ,
    "weather":[ {
        "id": 300, "main": "Drizzle", "description": "light intensity
drizzle", "icon": "09d"
    }
    ],
    "base":"stations",
    "main": {
        "temp": 280.32, "pressure": 1012, "humidity": 81, "temp_min":
279.15, "temp_max": 281.15
    }
    ,
    "visibility":10000,
    "wind": {
        "speed": 4.1, "deg": 80
    }
    ,
    "clouds": {
        "all": 90
    }
    ,
    "dt":1485789600,
    "sys": {
        "type": 1, "id": 5091, "message": 0.0103, "country": "GB",
"sunrise": 1485762037, "sunset": 1485794875
    }
    ,
    "id":2643743,
    "name":"London",
```

```
        "cod":200
    }
```

Now that the code is more, you can see that the data is displayed with an `id` and a `value`. We can use whichever we desire. For this exercise, we will pick the following data:

- Average Temperature
- Min Temperature
- Max Temperature
- The description of the weather
- The sunrise and sunset time

Let's get started.

The API call

First, we will need to create the HTML tag that will hold everything.

Let's create in our app an HTML tag `<weather>`:

```
<md-app-content>
        <!-- OUR APP HERE -->
        <weather></weather>
        </md-app-content>
```

In the `script` section, let's create our first Vue function:

```
Vue.component('weather', {
});
```

As we said earlier, we will need the data, the method, and the template to display the content. Let's start with the data:

```
Vue.component('weather', {

    data: function(){
            return {
                weatherLocation: '',
                weatherApi: '05911854df7aa0be884df72549a75fd9',
                weather: [],
                displayWeather: false
            }
```

```
        },

});
```

The function will store the following things:

- The location set by the user
- Our API Key
- The data pulled out from the API
- A boolean set to display or not display the information

Next, we will need to add the method, as follows:

```
methods: {
            getWeather: function()
            {
                return
this.$http.get('http://api.openweathermap.org/data/2.5/weather?q='+
this.weatherLocation +'&appid=' + this.weatherApi).then((response) => {
                    this.weather = response.body;
                    this.displayWeather = true
                }, (response) => {
                    this.weather = [];
                    this.displayWeather = false
                });
            }
        },
```

We will set the getWeather function, which will do the following things:

- Call the API with our API key and the location set by the user by the preceding data
- Store the data pulled from the API and set the display information to true
- If there is no answer or content from the API, the display information will be set to false

Finally, the template will be the following:

```
template: '<div id="weatherApp">' +
                '<form v-on:submit.prevent="getWeather"><md-field> <md-
icon>place</md-icon> <label>Location</label> <md-input type="text"
name="weatherLocation" v-model="weatherLocation"></md-input></md-field>' +
                '<md-button class="md-primary md-raised"
type="submit">Search</md-button> '+
                '</p>' +
```

```
                    '</form>' +
                    '<div v-if="displayWeather" class="container display-
weather-section"><md-card><md-card-header><h1>{{ weather.name }}</h1></md-
card-header>' +
                    '<md-card-content><weather-display v-
bind:weatherDisplay="weather.weather[0]"></weather-display>' +
                    '<temperature v-
bind:temperature="weather.main"></temperature>' +
                    '<clouds v-bind:cloud="weather.clouds"></clouds>' +
                    '<sun v-bind:sun="weather.sys"></sun>' +
                    '</md-card-content></md-card>' +
                    '</div></div>'

        });
```

Then, we will pass these pieces of information to a template we create for each. For the weather name and description, we have the following template:

```
Vue.component('weather-display', {
        props: ['weatherDisplay'],

        template: '<div id="weatherDisplay">' +
                    '<h2>{{ weatherDisplay.main }}</h2>' +
                    '<p>{{ weatherDisplay.description }}</p>' +
                    '</div>'
        });
```

We use the `props` property to pass the data and the `template` property to create the HTML with the value.

Then, we have the temperature. We will display the average temperature, maximum temperature, and minimum temperature. The data we get from OpenWeather API is in the format of Kelvin, so we need to create a function to convert the temperature.

To convert Kelvin to Celsius, you simply need to subtract 273.15 from the number:

```
Vue.component('temperature', {
        props: ['temperature'],

        methods: {
            displayTemp: function( temp )
            {
                return parseFloat(temp - 273.15).toFixed(2);
            }
        },

        template: '<div id="temp">' +
```

```
                        '<h2>Temperature</h2>' +
                        '<p>Avg Temp - {{ displayTemp(temperature.temp)
}}c</p>' +
                        '<p>Min Temp - {{ displayTemp(temperature.temp_min)
}}c</p>' +
                        '<p>Max Temp - {{ displayTemp(temperature.temp_max)
}}c</p>' +
                        '</div>'
        });
```

For the `cloud`, we simply need to display the text:

```
Vue.component('clouds', {
        props: ['cloud'],

        template: '<div id="cloud">' +
                        '<h2>Clouds</h2>' +
                        '<p>Coverage - {{ cloud.all }}%</p>' +
                        '</div>'
        });
```

Finally, we have the sunrise and sunset. The format we get from OpenWeather is in timestamp though, so we will need to convert it to date time:

```
Vue.component('sun', {
        props: ['sun'],

        methods: {
            timestampToDate: function( timestamp ){
                var date = new Date(timestamp*1000);
                return date.toString();
            }
        },

        template: '<div id="sun">' +
                        '<h2>Sun</h2>' +
                        '<p>Sunrise - {{ timestampToDate(sun.sunrise) }}</p>' +
                        '<p>Sunset - {{ timestampToDate(sun.sunset) }}</p>' +
                    '</div>'
        });
```

Our app is now finalized. Let's check out how it looks:

Our weather application - The Search bar

Then, we have our result page:

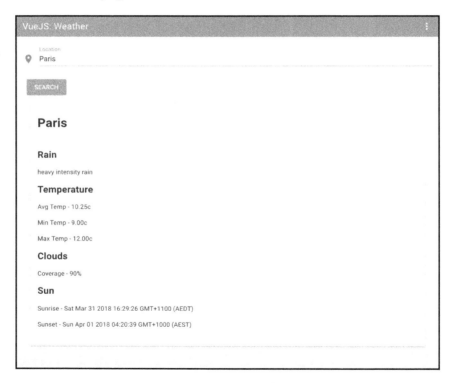

Our weather application - The Result page

Summary

This was a brief introduction to VueJS. There are so much more possibilities with this framework, and I've just touched a very small part of it. I hope this will bring you the curiosity to dig more into VueJS or whichever client-side rendering framework you choose. In the next final chapter, I will show you a list of tools that I use every day to help me with my workflow. These will surely help you as well. Let's jump into it!

Tools to Help Your Workflow **14**

What is a photographer without a camera or a fashion designer without a paper and pencil? As they say, you are only as good as your tools.

In this chapter, we will go over some of my favorite tools that should help you improve your workflow each day, such as the following:

- HTML Boilerplate
- Lorem Ipsum
- CSS preprocessor –Less
- CSS preprocessor – Sass
- ColorZilla
- Foundation
- Fontastic
- webflow
- Modernizr
- CSS3 Generator
- git
- Codekit
- Animate.css
- TinyPNG
- Unsplash

Let's get started!

HTML Boilerplate

We've already used this tool in our project. HTML5 Boilerplate is one of the top frontend templates available. As its name suggests, this frontend template is based on HTML5. It is a collection of libraries and hacks and enables you to get started quickly (and efficiently) with your newest project. HTML5 Boiler is perhaps the quickest solution to get your project up and running:

HTML Boilerplate

Whether you'd like to build websites or apps, you can use HTML5 Boilerplate to save time without compromising on performance.

What's even better about HTML5 Boilerplate is its huge community of support on GitHub. You can always find the help you need in the rare case that you encounter a problem. Although HTML5 Boilerplate isn't good for large-scale projects, it is perfect when you need to get started immediately with a smaller project and don't want to get bogged down with coding from scratch.

Lorem Ipsum

All of us are familiar with Lorem Ipsum, even if we don't know it by name. Designers use it as a way to simulate text in a design project.

In fact, Lorem Ipsum has been around for a lot longer than you think. It's not a new designer trick. The print and design industries have used this Latin text for the last 500 years to replicate the look of actual text:

Lorem Ipsum

However, you may be wondering, why Lorem Ipsum? Why use a dead language to fill a space when you could just as easily copy and paste a phrase like *your text here* over and over again?

Lorem Ipsum isn't just a filler text, it also provides an illusion. In content, just like what you're reading here, there is variation. You'll have two-letter words next to nine-letter words. There is no repeating pattern.

However, when you use a repeated phrase as your text placeholder, it can taint the entire project. The human eye will get distracted by the repeating pattern. This, of course, will pull attention away from your overall design and potentially cause the client to focus on all the nitpicky things that look off about the project.

If you're a purist, you can use Designers Toolbox's Lorem Ipsum (Greeking) Generator (`http://designerstoolbox.com/designresources/greek/`) here. It's perfect for a traditional Lorem Ipsum text placeholder. However, for a fun, humorous twist, check out Bacon Ipsum (`https://baconipsum.com/`).

CSS preprocessor – LESS

Want to do more with **Leaner Style Sheets** (**LESS**)? It's a language extension for CSS and one of the most popular CSS preprocessors available:

LESS

If you're already familiar with CSS, getting started with LESS will be easy for you. In fact, with a background in CSS, you could probably learn LESS in less time than it actually takes you to read the rest of this chapter.

So, why go with LESS instead of CSS? One of the biggest reasons to use LESS is that you can gain more time during your projects.

It works a lot like a programming language. Variables can be defined with LESS with an @ sign. Then, you can store a constant value that you can then reuse throughout your stylesheet. It's definitely a tool worth checking out.

CSS preprocessor – SCSS

LESS isn't the only CSS extension available. Check out **syntactically awesome style sheets** (**SASS**). It is a scripting language that's made up of two syntaxes: the original *indented syntax* (given the .sass extension) and the newer SCSS syntax (given the .scss extension):

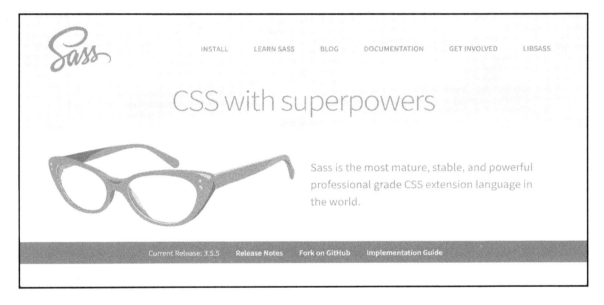

SCSS

No matter which version of CSS library you use, SASS is compatible with every one of them. Also, similar to LESS, SASS is open source and supported by a huge community of developers. Likewise, it's also backward compatible so that you can convert your CSS files.

So, why go with SASS over LESS? Depending on who you ask, SASS is much more popular and LESS is easier to use. It may boil down to whether you prefer Ruby or JavaScript. SASS is written in Ruby. However, LESS, which was originally written in Ruby, has ported to JavaScript. You'll need NodeJS to run LESS.

ColorZilla

Trying to find that perfect color but can't quite duplicate it?

Enter ColorZilla. This browser add-on is an eyedropper, a color picker, and a gradient generator. ColorZilla is available in both Chrome and Firefox. ColorZilla also offers a CSS gradient editor, which you can access directly from `http://www.colorzilla.com/gradient-editor/`:

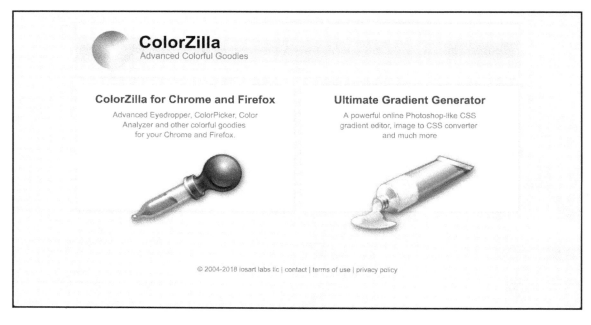

ColorZilla

For both graphic designers and web developers, ColorZilla is a lifesaver. It is a simple tool that you'll find yourself using every single day. It helps you to get an accurate color reading from any page (or image) in your browser.

Foundation

Created by Zurb, Foundation is an open source, responsive frontend framework.

Foundation is highly customizable. Designers prefer Foundation because it is compatible with almost every browser and device, adhering to the mobile-first mandate. When you need to set up a project quickly, including apps that must work on smartphones, Foundation is a smart choice. You don't need to know or tinker with backend coding. It simply works well for all types of projects, from prototypes to HTML emails to working websites:

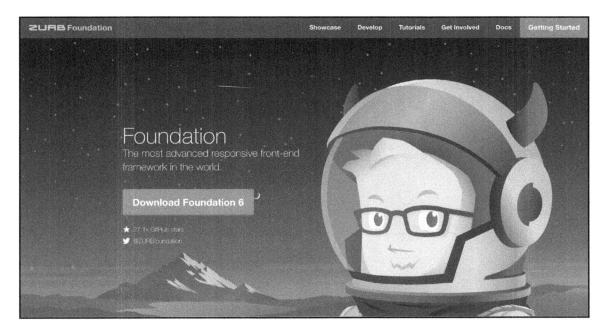

Foundation

Foundation can work with any CMS of your choice.

Fontastic

Ever needed to quickly change size or colors of your icons? What about adding shadows or other design elements to your icons?

Let's meet Fontastic. This fantastic tool allows designers to quickly change icons to meet the unique demands of any project. You can do this by creating your own icon font. Then, upload that font to your project. Once uploaded, you can use CSS to customize the look and feel of the icons without painstakingly manipulating each icon in Photoshop:

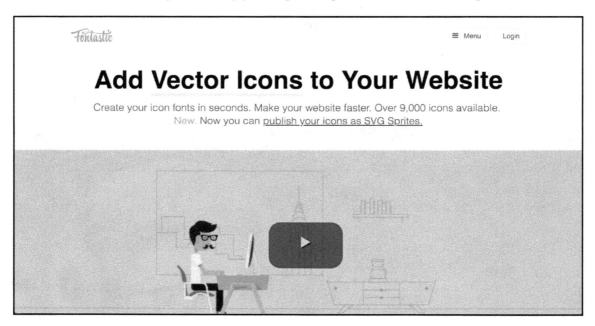

Fontastic (http://fontastic.me/)

Here's how it works. Head over to Fontastic and select icons from its huge library of over 9,000 available icon images. Next, assign letters to each of those icons (to create a font).

From there, you can modify your icons with the help of CSS. From changing color to resizing, you can do all of it through coding instead of redrawing and wasting a lot of time.

webflow

Good news—you can still design and build websites even if you don't know much at all about coding.

webflow is just the tool that you need. It is a half designer, half develop, and fully amazing. You can visually set up your website design and then webflow does the rest. It will code your website to come to life and function flawlessly:

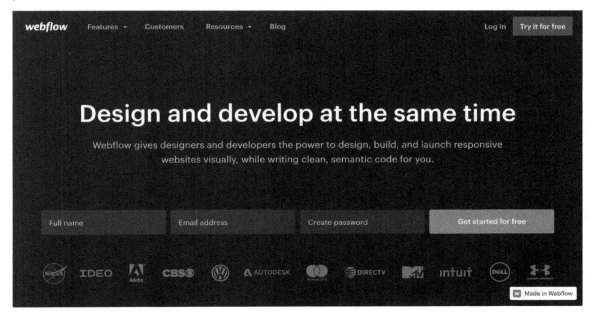

webflow (https://webflow.com/)

No mocks and no prototypes here. webflow creates live and fully functional websites that use HTML, CSS, and JavaScript.

By the way, did I mention that it's responsive too? That means that you don't have to worry about the final project looking wonky on smaller viewing screens.

In case you're wondering about the quality of the code, you can rest assured that webflow guarantees clean code that won't slow down the site visitor's experience.

Modernizr

Modernizr is a small JavaScript library that's used to automatically detect features and/or technologies (such as HTML5) in your user's browser. The purpose of this tool is to optimize your website user's experience based on their unique browser. You can use Modernizr to offer a pleasant browsing experience on your site, no matter how new or outdated the browser is:

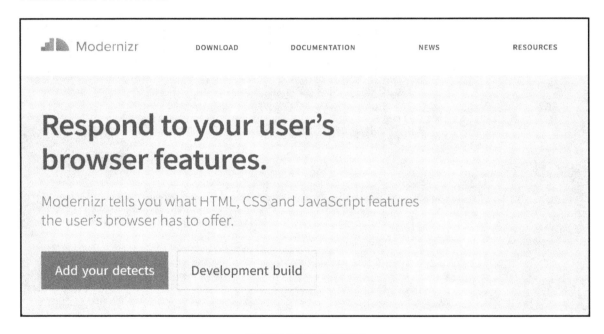

ModerniZR (https://modernizr.com/)

CSS3 Generator

When you need to quickly create code for your CSS, you will need a CSS3 Generator.

From text shadows to gradients, from multiple columns to transitions, you can do a lot with a simple CSS3 Generator:

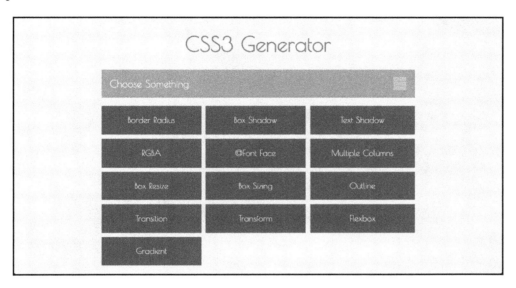

CSS3 Generator (http://css3generator.com/)

The good news is that CSS3 Generators has a lot of tools to help you. Generate your CSS3 snippet through one of their tools and then copy the code directly into your project. Coding isn't for everyone, and if you're more of a visual thinker, this generator shortcut is the perfect solution for you.

CSS3 Generator is one of my favorite CSS3 tools because it's fast, clean, and easy to use.

git

Are all of the following true for you:

- You need a version control system to track any changes made to your files
- You work with many people
- You need to work either remotely or offline frequently

Then, you need git:

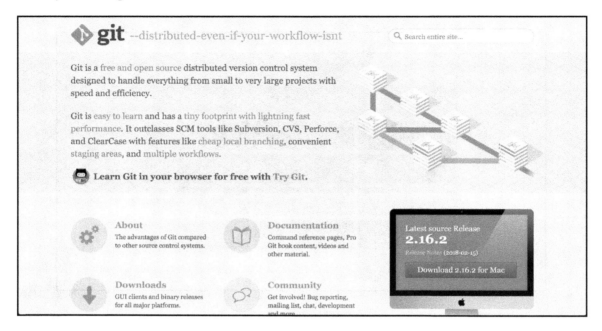

git (https://git-scm.com/)

The git is an open source version control system. Whether you are working on a small project or a huge one, git is a good option. Its speed and flexibility make it an awesome choice.

Here's how git works:

git works with your local copy and can be performed when you're offline:

1. Whenever you save your work, git creates an image of your files, also known as a commit
2. Each time this commit is created, it links to your other commits, which means that there's a change of all activities on your files
3. Whenever you (or someone else on your team) make changes, your commit creates a record of it
4. You can use this to reverse changes and return to a previous commit

Another benefit of git is how files are handled. Files exist as modified, staged, or committed. In the modified state, the change you've made to the file only exists in your local, working directory. You can then stage those newly modified files. The final stage is committed when changes become a permanent part of the file's development.

CodeKit

CodeKit is another tool for building websites. Basically, CodeKit automates a lot of developer tasks so that building a website doesn't take forever. It compiles any and every language, so CodeKit is incredibly easy to work with:

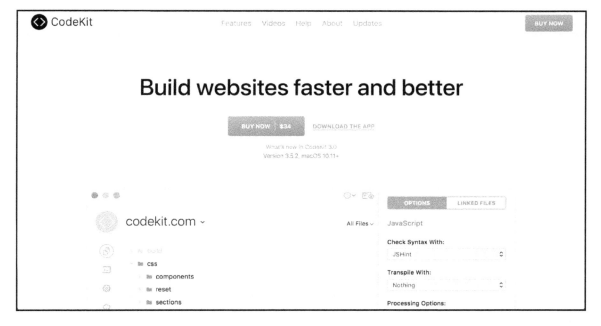

CodeKit (https://codekitapp.com/)

I love CodeKit for the simple reason that you don't have to refresh your browser after changes. CodeKit automatically does it for you. All browsers are supported, all devices are supported.

Another reason to drop everything and go CodeKit? Site optimization is so easy. CodeKit allows you to minimize your images by up to 70 percent in one click. You can use it to minify scripts and reduce HTTP requests. These types of optimizations are some of the best ways to ensure a speedy website.

CodeKit's drag and drop user interface is slick and friendly.

Animate.css

Animate.CSS is pretty much just for fun. From attention seekers to zoom exits, you'll find dozens of CSS animations to spruce up your web design:

Animate CSS (https://daneden.github.io/animate.css/)

Animate.CSS comes packaged in one tiny file. Everything you need is contained in that file. After downloading it from the official website, you'll drop the stylesheet into the head of your document. From there, you'll add the animation of your choice to the desired element and watch with glee as your ideas pop off the screen (or whichever effect you've chosen). It's all documented in a README file
at `(https://github.com/daneden/animate.css/blob/master/README.md)`.

Animate.CSS is a great option for adding delight and interest to your web project. Since it's CSS, it's lightweight and compatible with most viewing screens.

TinyPNG

One of my absolute favorite designer tools is TinyPNG. As its name suggests, TinyPNG compresses a PNG or JPEG image to reduce the file size. However, it does so without degrading the visual quality of your files—it's like magic:

TinyPNG (https://tinypng.com/)

To achieve maximum speed for your web projects, it's important to reduce file size wherever possible. There's little doubt that image files are often the biggest files on a website. This is why: TinyPNG is an amazing option—it reduces your file sizes (often by 50 percent or more) without compromising on visuals. Smaller file sizes not only equal faster loading times but also save your bandwidth.

TinyPNG is lightning fast to use, and if you sign up for a Pro account, you can upload up to 25 MB at one time. With the free service, you are limited to 20 images with a maximum of 5 MB each.

Unsplash

When you need a quality photo, but can't afford to pay photo a photographer, or just need a placeholder for some design, Unsplash (`https://unsplash.com/`) is for you. It provides open source and free-to-use images uploaded by photographers:

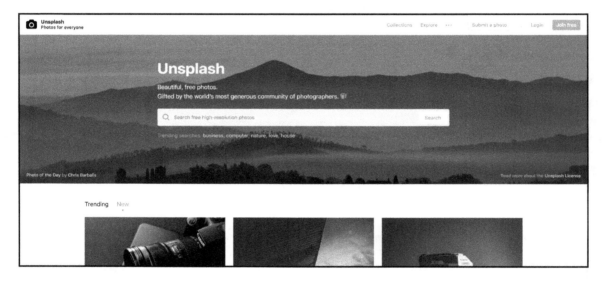

Unsplash (https://unsplash.com/)

I use it every day, and, to be honest, it became one of the websites I use the most.

Summary

I hope this list of tools will help you like it helps me. Use it without moderation. The good thing about the design community is that everyone likes to share their work and help one other. Designers and developers are an open community, and that is the real spirit of our community.

Other Books You May Enjoy

If you enjoyed this book, you may be interested in these other books by Packt:

Responsive Web Design by Example
Frahaan Hussain

ISBN: 978-1-78728-706-8

- Understand what responsive design is, and why it's vital for modern web development
- Customize and extend responsive design frameworks
- Create adaptable templates for all future projects
- Build a semantic website structure with HTML5 elements
- Determine a responsive website persona with CSS3
- Learn how to decide which framework best suits your project specification
- Implement a plethora of Bootstrap features in your websites

Hands-On Data Structures and Algorithms with JavaScript
Kashyap Mukkamala

ISBN: 978-1-78839-855-8

- Build custom Back buttons embedded within your application
- Build part of a basic JavaScript syntax parser and evaluator for an online IDE
- Build a custom activity user tracker for your application
- Generate accurate recommendations for credit card approval using Decision Trees
- Simplify complex problems using a graph data structure based on the application
- Increase the performance of an application using micro-optimizations

Leave a review - let other readers know what you think

Please share your thoughts on this book with others by leaving a review on the site that you bought it from. If you purchased the book from Amazon, please leave us an honest review on this book's Amazon page. This is vital so that other potential readers can see and use your unbiased opinion to make purchasing decisions, we can understand what our customers think about our products, and our authors can see your feedback on the title that they have worked with Packt to create. It will only take a few minutes of your time, but is valuable to other potential customers, our authors, and Packt. Thank you!

Index

9

960 grid system
  reference 18

A

About us section
  creating 156, 157, 158, 159, 160, 161, 162
  creating, as responsive 198, 199
  styling 295, 296, 297
adaptive design
  about 73, 74
  comparing, with responsive design 76, 77
  drawbacks 77
  examples 75, 76
  pros and cons 78
Animate.css
  about 342, 343
  reference 342
Atom
  about 79
  URL 79
  using 79, 80
attributes 82

B

block element
  about 99, 100
  examples 100
Blog section
  creating 147, 148, 149, 151, 152, 153
  creating, as responsive 195, 196, 197
  styling 287, 289, 292, 293, 294
Bootstrap
  about 255, 256, 258
  components 259, 260, 261, 262

Grid system 263, 264, 265
Hero section, styling 284, 285, 286, 287
installing 270, 271
media queries 266, 267
navbar, creating 273, 274
navigation bar, styling 280, 281, 282, 283
navigation, coding 275, 276, 277, 278, 280
project, setting up 271, 272, 273
reference 259
URL 255, 271
Bracket
  URL 79
Breadcrumb
  about 32
  example 33

C

Call to Action (CTA)
  about 27
  compelling copy 30
  contrasting color, using 29
  example 28
  obvious design 27
  placement 31, 32
Cascading Style Sheet (CSS)
  about 14, 15, 91
  child element 93
  classes 94, 95, 96, 97
  curly bracket 92
  dividers 101
  formatting 92
  IDs 94, 95, 96, 97
  layout 101
  parent element 93
  property 92
  pseudo-class 203, 204, 205, 206

selector 92
semicolon 92
using 91, 92
value 92
casual scripts 46
child element 93
classes
about 94, 95, 96, 97
versus IDs 94
client-side rendering
about 305, 306
pros and cons 307
CodeKit 341, 342
colors
meanings 50, 52
reference 296
using 50
ColorZilla
about 334, 335
URL 334
consistency
about 55
in content 57
in design 56
in interactions 57
Content Delivery Network (CDN) 271
contract samples
reference 62
CSS animation
creating 211, 212
CSS box model
about 97
block element 99, 100, 101
inline element 99, 100, 101
properties 97, 99
CSS flexbox
using 141, 142
CSS position values
about 143
absolute 144
fixed 145
relative 144
static 144
sticky 146
CSS3 Generator 338, 339

D

dividers, CSS 101
domain name
buying 244, 245, 246, 248, 249, 250
Dreamweaver
URL 79
dynamic Instagram feed
access token, obtaining 219, 221, 222
adding 213, 214
displaying 223, 224, 225, 226, 228, 229, 230, 231
images, obtaining from user account 216
Instafeed.js, installing 215, 216
TokenAccess, searching 217, 219
userID, searching 217, 219

E

elements, HTML
about 83
images, adding 86, 87, 88
links, adding 86, 87, 88
paragraphs, adding 83, 84, 85, 86
titles, inserting 83, 84, 85, 86

F

Facebook like button
URL 124
favicon generator
URL 234
favicon
creating 233, 234, 235
Figma 112
File Transfer Protocol (FTP) 246
FileZilla
URL 246
Flash
about 12, 14
reference 13
URL 13
flat design 19, 20, 21
Fontastic 336
fonts
casual scripts 46
installing, for web page 118, 119

reference 49
sans-serif 45
selecting 44
serif 44
footer section
  adding 168, 169, 170
  creating, as responsive 200, 201
  styling 299, 301, 302
Foundation 335

G

git 339, 340
goal identification
  about 59
  brand identity, creating 61
  competitors, identifying 61, 62
  customers information, gathering 60
  Information Architecture (IA), defining 60
  target audience, identifying 60
  website purpose, identifying 60
Google Analytics
  about 250
  using 251, 253
Google Font
  importing 120
  URL 49, 120
Google Search Console
  about 253
  URL 253
  using 254
Grid system, Bootstrap 263, 264, 265
grids
  about 24
  cons 25, 26, 27
  reference 289

H

header
  Facebook like button, adding 124, 125
  implementing 121
  links, inserting 122
  logo, adding 123, 124
  menu, creating 121
  right-hand side menu, creating 124

styling 126, 128, 129, 130, 131, 132, 133, 134
Hero section
  adding 135, 136, 137, 138, 139, 140
  creating, as responsive 194, 195
  CSS flexbox, using 141, 142, 143
  CSS position values 143
  styling, with Bootstrap 284, 285, 286, 287
home page
  design 111, 112, 113
HTML Boilerplate
  about 330
  index.html, editing 115, 116, 117
  installing 113, 114
  URL 113
Hypertext Markup Language (HTML)
  about 79, 81
  attributes 82
  elements 83
  page, creating 82, 83
  structure 82
  tags 81

I

icons
  about 37
  describing 38
  directional 40
  users attention, drawing 38, 39, 40
IDs
  about 94, 95, 96, 97
  versus classes 94
images
  adding 86, 87, 88
Information Architecture (IA) 60
inline element
  about 99, 100
  examples 101
Instafeed.js
  installing 215, 216
  URL 215

J

JavaScript plugins
  Google Analytics 117

Jquery 117
Main.js 117
modernizr 117
Plugin.js 117
jQuery
  about 188
  syntax 189, 191, 192, 193

L

layout, CSS
  about 101
  class, styling 102, 103, 104, 105, 106, 108,
    109, 110
  creating 101
  HTML, formatting 102
  HTML, indenting 102
Leaner Style Sheets (LESS) 332, 333
links
  adding 86, 87, 88
Lorem Ipsum 331

M

media queries 267
  about 18, 174, 175, 266, 267
  desktop design, starting 178
  inspector, opening 175, 177, 178
menu
  designing 179, 180, 181, 182, 183, 184, 185,
    186, 187
Minifier
  URL 238
mobile browsing 17, 18
mobile first 76
modal box
  about 40
  examples 41, 42
  usages 41
Modernizr 338

N

Namecheap 245
navbar
  creating 273, 274
navigation bar

styling 280, 281, 282, 283

O

OpenWeather
  URL 320

P

page
  creating 82, 83
paragraphs
  adding 83, 84, 85, 86
parent element 93
Partners section
  adding 163, 164, 165, 166, 168
  styling 298, 299
performance optimization, website
  about 236
  code, optimizing 238, 239
  images, optimizing 237, 238
project designing
  design, improving 66
  design, inventing 66
  framework, using 66
  inspiration, obtaining 66
project scope
  defining 62
properties, CSS box model
  border 97
  content 97
  margin 97
  padding 97
pseudo-class
  about 204
  URL 206
  using 204, 205, 206

R

Racing Club project 59
responsive design
  about 70, 71
  comparing, with adaptive design 76, 77
  examples 72, 73
  pros and cons 78
responsive web design

about 18, 19
reference 19
Roboto font
  URL 120

S

sans-serif fonts 45
search bar
  about 34
  customizing 35, 36
  placing, correctly 37
  submit button 34
search engine optimization (SEO)
  about 12, 240
  improvement 239
  keywords 244
  links 244
  meta description 240, 241
  valid HTML 241, 242, 243
serif fonts 44
server-side rendering
  about 305
  pros and cons 306
Sketch app
  about 112
  URL 112
sticky navigation
  building 206, 207, 208
  CSS animation, creating 211, 212
  Waypoints, using 209, 210, 211
Sublime Text 3
  URL 79
syntactically awesome style sheets (SASS) 333

T

table-based layouts 10, 11, 12
tags 81
text editor
  Atom 79
The Grid system
  URL 25
TinyPNG 343
titles
  inserting 83, 84, 85, 86

typography
  about 43, 44
  font, selecting 44
  multiple typefaces, avoiding 46, 49

U

Unminify
  URL 239
Unsplash
  about 344
  URL 344
usability
  about 52
  accessibility 54
  availability 54
  navigability 53
  simplicity 53
User Interface (UI) 56
UXPin
  URL 77

V

Vue Material
  URL 315
  using 315, 316, 317
VueJS
  about 307, 308
  setting up 309, 310, 311, 312, 313, 314
  URL 309
  weather application, creating 314

W

W3 markup validator
  about 241
  URL 241
Waypoints
  URL 209
  using 209, 210, 211
weather application
  API call, managing 322, 323, 324, 325, 326
  components 317
  creating, in VueJS 314
  OpenWeather API, accessing 318, 319, 320, 321, 322

Vue Material, using 315, 316, 317
Web 2.0 16, 17
web design
  evolution 22
  Racing Club project 59
web page
  creating 117
  font, installing 118, 119
  Google Font, importing 120
  images folder, using 118
  normalize.css, adding 121
webflow 337
website

domain name, buying 244, 245, 246, 248, 249, 250
history 8, 9, 10
implementing 68
launching 68, 244
performance optimization 236
testing 68
wireframes
  creating 62, 64, 65
World Wide Web (WWW) 8
WWW Consortium (W3C)
  about 9
  URL 9

www.ingramcontent.com/pod-product-compliance
Lightning Source LLC
Chambersburg PA
CBHW080614060326
40690CB00021B/4691